Fundraising for Volunteers

Including

The ONE Secret Key to Fundraising Success

BRIAN TURNER

BALBOA.
PRESS
A DIVISION OF HAY HOUSE

Balboa Press books may be ordered through booksellers or by contacting:

Balboa Press
A Division of Hay House
1663 Liberty Drive
Bloomington, IN 47403
www.balboapress.com.au
1-(877) 407-4847

ISBN: 978-1-4525-0817-7 (sc)
ISBN: 978-1-4525-0818-4 (e)

Printed in the United States of America

Balboa Press rev. date: 11/22/2012

Contents

Preface

Volunteer fundraisers are everywhere in our community.

People from all over Australia are volunteering to run fundraising events with the aim of raising much needed funds to help the worthy causes they care about. The list of organisations that run fundraising events is quite a large one. Groups that fundraise include sporting clubs, service clubs, church groups, health groups, education groups, scouts/girl guides, lifesavers, bowls/golf clubs, disadvantaged interest groups, disabled interest groups, industry groups and many more. Essentially any group with a community interest will fundraise at some time. If you participate in your community in any way it is likely that you have, or one day will, find yourself in the role of a volunteer fundraiser.

There are two types of fundraisers to be aware of. Firstly there are the professional fundraisers who are paid either part time, full time, or on contract to raise funds for their employer who is usually a Not For Profit organisation of some sort. These people usually have a great deal of experience across a broad range of fundraising activities.

However professional fundraisers are far outnumbered by the second type of fundraiser—the volunteer. There are many times more volunteer fundraisers than paid fundraisers. Volunteers are usually members of a club, committee or group of some kind although they don't necessarily have to be. Some may be quite experienced in fundraising but most commonly volunteers have a limited knowledge about fundraising and make up for it with motivation and enthusiasm.

According to research undertaken by Philanthropy Australia[1], the estimated number of people in Australia aged 18 years and over who volunteer is 4,395,600, and this represents 32% of the civilian population.

The most frequent activities that volunteers undertake are;

Activity	Frequency
Fundraising	56%
Management	45%
Teaching	44%
Administration	41%

These figures show that 56% of all adult volunteers, or 2,461,536 people, undertake volunteering to raise funds in Australia each year. This equates to 18% or nearly one in five of all adults in Australia that volunteer as fundraisers each year.

To put this figure into perspective let's compare it with figures from the Australian Bureau of Statistics for some other industries.

The Retail Trade industry employs 1,211,332 people and the Manufacturing industry employs 1,010,179 people[2]. These are Australia's two largest industries and combined these two industries employ just 16% of all adults in Australia. This demonstrates just exactly how big the volunteer industry is and exactly how predominant volunteer fundraising is in our country.

With all these people involved in fundraising, you may be tempted to think that volunteer fundraisers would be well supported with plenty of information and advice in a very mature industry. Well hardly! Because the nature of volunteering means there is no payment for the work done, volunteers often find themselves working for organisations that have an obligation to strictly contain costs. This leads to the situation where volunteers are often not provided with the training or support that a paid staff member in a commercial organisation might receive.

Volunteer fundraisers are usually very committed to the cause and are willing to make substantial efforts to help. However they also often report they need more support and guidance in order to become more effective with their fundraising activities. They want to be more effective so they can raise more money for their cause.

This book provides volunteers with the knowledge that can turn novice fundraisers into confident fundraisers with the ability to turn a vague fundraising idea into an organisational and financial success.

It contains information which will help experienced volunteer fundraisers improve their current fundraising events and find new fundraising events which could provide exciting new income streams for their organisation.

Everybody who reads this book will broaden their knowledge and experience with fundraising activities.

Introduction

I guess my involvement with fundraising started when I was a teenager growing up in the suburbs of Melbourne. Like most teenagers, I was keen to find a little extra money to spend on whatever teenagers spend their money on. I heard that you could get paid a small amount of money if you collected used beer bottles and sold them back to the breweries. So I went around my local streets and asked my neighbours if I could have their empty beer bottles. I would regularly collect these discarded beer bottles, bring them home on a small home-made trolley and store them up behind the family garage. Once a year I would phone the depot and they would come and collect them and leave me a cheque for my efforts. This just seemed too easy to me but I had luckily stumbled on an easy way to fundraise which suited my abilities and resources.

Later in life as a young adult, I discovered the added joys of fundraising for charity instead of fundraising for myself. Since then I have been involved with more than 10 different organisations that fundraise and have spent over 30 years gaining experience in the fundraising industry in virtually every role that could be imagined. I have found a great career within the fundraising industry working as a professional fundraiser with some of Australia's blue chip not-for-profit organisations. I have been very lucky to work with so many wonderful volunteers and working with kind hearted community minded people brings me genuine and deep enjoyment.

Through my work over the years in the fundraising industry, I have come to recognise there are essentially four different conditions that can exist within fundraising groups.

First is the situation where an eager and enthusiastic committee have no idea what event to run.

Second is the situation where an eager and enthusiastic committee have a fundraising idea which they are really attached to and excited about (because it is their idea) but in reality it is quite unlikely to work.

In the third situation a small group of people are undertaking all of the demanding roles of running the fundraising events and need new, active people to join with them to continue achieving the results they currently enjoy.

Finally, the fourth situation is where the organisation has a series of successful events which are run quite capably by a large group of very committed people.

Whilst we all aim to be part of the fourth group, only few groups ever attain this status. The first three situations prevail in most groups. Even in groups where the fourth situation clearly exists, the members can still drop back to one of the first three situations at various times as well.

It is the goal of this book to move all fundraising committees into the fourth category. To achieve this I have arranged this book into three logical sections.

Section1 will help you get a committee together and give you some guidance in how to manage it. It covers everything you need to know to lead a fundraising organisation and get a great result from your fundraising activity. It includes chapters on the topics of forming the committee, allocating roles, running the committee and identifying the benefits of fundraising events. Too often I have seen really worthy fundraising events fail because the committee lacked some small ingredient in some small way. Section 1 will help with this problem.

Section 2 will help you with selecting an appropriate fundraising event that suits your group in your local area. It contains a very simple but significant single 'key to success' for running fundraising activities. This key was designed to be so simple that you can easily remember it and carry it around with you in your head at all times. You will be able to refer to it in committee meetings particularly when you are selecting a new fundraising event for your group to run.

Section 3 provides some assistance with the actual staging of the event. It contains chapters on the topics of event planning, uncontrollable occurrences, supervision, and celebrating the results.

The appendixes contain examples of documents necessary for your committee to make staging events easier and less demanding and they will help to make your event more successful this year and also in the long term.

One of the most common situations I have seen in many volunteer fundraising groups is that they fall into category 1 above. They have an eager and enthusiastic committee but have no idea what event to run. Their challenge is to find an appropriate fundraising activity that would suit their particular group in their particular town. Appendix 1 will help with event selection by providing a comprehensive listing of fundraising activities for you to select from once you have a good committee together and a good understanding of the secret key. It is a compendium of fundraising activities that any committee can pick up at any time to find a new event which suits their group and their resources. I have included enough information about each event to help committees make an informed decision about which event to run that suits the level of their resources.

Volunteer fundraising committees are quite commonly made up of very practical people. They want to get the job done without too much bureaucracy, tedious processes or procedures. Whilst fundraising events do require processes and procedures, this book incorporates them into a no nonsense straight forward manner that will really get results. It has been written for volunteer committees of all experience and capability levels.

Please read on and enjoy learning about fundraising for volunteers and may all your events and activities be financially successful, provide other meaningful benefits to your group, and be rewarding for you personally to run.

SECTION 1

The Committee

Chapter 1

Forming The Committee

There's a common saying that goes, "You can't run a business by committee". This may be so, but committees are the preferred way of running fundraising events. Using a committee structure to run fundraising events is done primarily because of the cost savings of using volunteers. At the same time, using a committee provides the benefit of utilising many people's individual skills and sharing the work between more people. I think everyone would be aware that there are downsides to committees and some that I can think of are that they are often cumbersome, slow, ineffectual, confrontational and poorly focused. Of course all of these same criticisms can be made of any management style in the wrong hands. Anyway like it or not, the committee structure is firmly entrenched as the common management structure for running fundraising events and our task is to make the committee structure work the best that it can.

Recruiting New Members
Many volunteer groups believe that recruiting new committee members is an impossible task and their despair begins here. I would like you to believe that there are <u>always</u> people who are willing to join your committee and help. It is just a matter of finding them. If you know where and how to look for new members you will find new people who value your cause and the benefits that come from joining in. Some people may find this hard to accept, but it is true.

Here are some tips for looking for new members for your committee. Look for;

- people who have a personal interest in your cause,
- people who can be educated about your cause,
- people that have a proven track record with committees, events or in business,
- people who have a 'can do' attitude,
- people who can 'get on' with other people, and
- people you or other committee members already know.

I think we've all heard the common saying; "If you want something done then give it to a busy person." Whilst this can be true and I have seen it work with some remarkable results, equally I have seen people who appear almost idle achieve some remarkable results. Therefore it is not how busy people are that increases their likelihood of success. What it comes down to, is finding people who value your cause and the benefits highly enough.

When recruiting members there are two types of people to consider:

Type 1—The Busy
These are the people who are already undertaking a huge amount of activity in their lives, ie. they are busy and feel like they couldn't fit anything else in. These people are time poor. When approaching these people talk about the benefits your organisation offers to them personally, their family and their community. Often these people can rearrange their priorities to fit an extra commitment in when they understand how important the cause is to them. They may well be looking for a reason to drop something else out of their life that doesn't bring them the rewards your fundraising event could.

With these people it is wise to encourage them to only take on small tasks at first. As things change in their lives and a little more time becomes available, these 'busy' people will want to fill it up with something. This can lead to these people contributing much higher levels of involvement as time progresses.

I am without a doubt a 'Busy' and with every committee that I've ever joined I started as a simple member with a simple role. As I came to understand and appreciate the role of the organisation and the benefits to the community I became more committed to the organisation. This has led me to being more strongly involved and engaged, often eventually taking the role of Chair and in some cases for many years. As the Chair of a committee I usually seek to find new members, give them simple tasks and progress their engagement with the organisation at the pace that they are comfortable with. Thus the circle of life continues for the committee and it will be refreshed regularly with new members.

Type 2—The Free

These are the people who have spare time on their hands and are willing if not eager, to find something to do to keep from being lonely and unchallenged. These people are time rich and are often retired, working part-time, unemployed or students. Calling them 'Free' just means they are time free.

These people will probably also be quiet when they first join the committee so allocating them a demanding task could be quite stressful for them. It's always a good idea to start new members off slowly and increase their task level in time as their engagement increases.

If you do get a 'Free' as a new member, they could well become a strong member who stays with the organisation for many years. Once fully engaged these people are often very reliable and long serving valuable participants on fundraising committees.

Finding either of these types of people will be quite difficult if you do not fit into the same category yourself. People generally choose to surround themselves with friends and acquaintances who are much like themselves. If you are a 'Busy' then your friends will probably be 'Busy' people as well. If you are a 'Free', your friends are likely to be 'Free' people also.

You can find these people by having a key person in one of these areas on your committee already. For example, a retiree who lives in a retirement village, attends seniors meetings and plays lawn bowls, should have more success at finding other 'Free' people than an employed person would. Enlist the help of a 'Free' person to help find other 'Free' people.

Similarly, if you are an Free and believe that your committee would benefit by having a 'Busy' member or two, then get a 'Busy' person to help you find these people.

I've always found that the personal approach is by far the most successful method of finding new volunteer members. Advertising may work for some high profile causes but even in these organisations the personal approach gets better results than advertising. Using the personal approach does not mean that you will have to recruit all the new members yourself. If you recruit two or three key people and then help them to recruit two or three themselves, very soon you will have a committee of ten or more people who all have a personal involvement with the key committee members.

Because I understand the natural delay that occurs after a new member joins the committee before they become fully active, I have learned to really enjoy the presence of members who do very little for the committee. They could well become a key person in the organisation in a year or two and exercising patience with them whilst they slowly become more engaged will pay dividends for many years.

Additionally, many people (but not all) who get involved in a committee will vary their involvement level over the years. In one club that I was a part of, we met over lunch once a week. I held major roles in eight of the ten years that I was involved with this club, but in the other two years I became what we called a "knife and fork" member, ie. one who came only for the meal. This did not mean that I was ready to leave the organisation, or that I was letting the team down during those years, simply that everyone needs a rest every now and then and it is imperative that all committee members understand this. Pressuring a member to increase their involvement during a rest period will not encourage them to remain loyal to the Chair or the organisation.

Engaging Members
Some Chairs think that once the new committee is formed the most important objective is to motivate the members to get started on the event, but this approach can cause problems. For many people motivation is something that exists for as long as it is provided to them and once it is removed they become demotivated and inactive.

There is something that is far better that motivating people, and that is engaging them. Engaged people will continue with their tasks even without the attention of someone to motivate them.

Therefore, once the committee is formed and meetings begun, the challenge for you is to get the committee members engaged. Just giving them a job will not usually do the trick to engage members. Each person is unique and brings certain talents to the committee but they also bring certain questions and doubts. To ensure that each member fully accepts their roles and engages with the committee, the Chairman will need to work carefully with each member individually.

This is best done on a personal level as it is very rare for a new member speak up in a meeting and say that they really don't think they can achieve their tasks. On a personal and informal level (perhaps after the meeting over a cup of tea) a quick and simple question like "Do you think that you'll need any extra help to get that job done?" will often bring up other concerns that weren't raised during the meeting. Solving these concerns at this point will encourage the new member to engage with their tasks and increase the likelihood of a successful outcome.

When the Chair of a committee is checking up with members about the progress of tasks outside of normal meetings, it can sometimes be seen like a boss checking up on an employee. The last thing that a volunteer committee member needs or wants is extra stress in their lives. Volunteers do not respond well to orders but do respond well to camaraderie and friendship, so keep discussions like these on the basis of being peers and equals.

I also suggest that all committee members have a role even if it means having a number of members work together on a single task. Leaving some members without any tasks at all disengages them and can also lead to other active members becoming disgruntled. If a member is having a rest year or is new to the committee and not yet fully engaged, they should have very simple tasks (perhaps as part of a sub group) but they should definitely have an allocated role.

Empowering Members
Once the committee has enough members who are engaged with the organisation and the event, the next step is to empower them. Empowered members will perform so much better than dis-empowered ones.

The easy way to empower a member is to not only give them a task but to also give them the responsibility for the task also. This would involve providing them with a certain latitude in making decisions within their portfolio.

For example, if Joan was in charge of printing the entry tickets to an event she should be allowed to go away and produce a series of ideas about the tickets and bring those ideas back to the committee for discussion.

However, if Joan was first told all the details and what the appearance of them was to be, which printer to use, and then told to go away and get the tickets organised, then she has diminished responsibility over the task and would certainly feel dis-empowered.

Empowered volunteers also are ones who are authorised with a certain level of decision making. Chairmen will need to ensure that empowered members who desire and have earned a level of independence, still remain operating within the guidelines of the committee. In the next Chapter I explain the attributes of a Chairman that would be needed to achieve this.

Chapter 2

Allocating Roles

Members of committees naturally have their own unique sets of skills and interests. A successful committee is one where the best use is made of each members particular skills and interests. If a person has a strong interest in finance then they would probably make a good treasurer. Likewise, if a person is a good organiser of people then they would probably make a good Chairman.

The interesting thing about a person's estimation of their own levels of their skills level, is that it is quite common for people to underestimate or overestimate their own abilities. I have found that about 90% of people on volunteer committees will underestimate their abilities which I believe is mostly due to the inbuilt unassuming nature of the general volunteer. Managed effectively, these volunteers will have the wonderful habit of achieving tasks they said they couldn't do and the committee will be warmly surprised by their results.

The 10% who overestimate their skills have the potential to cause significant harm to an event as they claim to be able to achieve something they really can't. The best course of action for the committee Chairman is to limit the tasks these people are allocated, and only allocate further tasks when the first ones are satisfactorily completed.

A person's estimation of their level of ability should not be confused with a person's willingness to engage. Engagement is a person's willingness to be involved and their ability is the skills they use to achieve outcomes.

One of the best ways to fit people into roles is to sit everyone down in a meeting environment and provide them with a detailed description of all the roles on the committee. You could then ask each person where they feel they would best fit in. You will almost certainly end up with some roles that have too many people and some roles that have too few. The beauty of volunteers is that you will almost certainly also have people on the committee who are willing to shift roles to fill in the gaps. If someone does take on a role that they are not really strong at, I usually make that role into a sub-committee where 2 or 3 people can work together to achieve the outcomes. The Chairman will have to keep a close eye on that role to ensure that the people involved are getting the support they need to get the job done.

In the first year of existence for a committee it is common for some members to be in roles that really don't suit them very well. As time progresses it is wise to move these people into positions they are better suited for.

All people have different attributes and I use a system to allocate people into one of two broad groups. Each person is either primarily people oriented or task oriented. It is my finding that all people will exhibit a primary orientation to one of these two styles. They may well be strongly or mildly located into one of these two groups and indeed some people do move between them, but all people have a way of operating in the world that is primarily task or people oriented.

People who are people oriented will commonly have a poor understanding of task oriented people who value the completion of the task above all else. Task oriented people will similarly have a poor understanding of people oriented people, who value the well being of other people above all else. With careful planning both these types of people can find a way to work well together.

Task oriented people are very good in roles like finance, secretary, and resource management. People oriented people are very good in roles like leadership, teamwork and customer relations. You can use this knowledge to help you allocate people to roles which suit their particular attributes.

Chapter 3

Running The Committee

There are two main tasks in being the President or Chairman of an organisation.

Firstly you must lead the team members and secondly you will most probably Chair the meetings. It is not usually written into Constitutions or By-Laws that the President must also Chair the meetings and in fact anyone could actually do this task. I've seen very successful meetings that were chaired by an ordinary member whilst the President sat beside them. However this is an exception and most volunteer committees meetings are chaired by the President. In this book when I refer to the Chair of the meeting I am also referring to the President of the organisation.

All committees have a requirement for accountability to its members, supporters and the general public, so some committee processes must absolutely be adhered to and others may be flexible and open to adapting. I've chaired many fundraising committees where a formal meeting structure was adhered to and I've also chaired other committees which were so informal they did not have an agenda, make any motions, or take any minutes. Both types of committees were structured to suit the people involved and the events we were running and both types were successful. If I had tried to change the process in either situation the committee members would have rejected the changes or refused to participate.

Often, committees without structure are small groups of friends who come together with an idea for an event and then approach a community organisation with an offer to run the event and then donate the proceeds to them. They are not part of the community organisation and do not want to be bound by formal processes. This occurs quite frequently with volunteer fundraisers and results speak for themselves. If a loose gathering of people who meet over a cuppa can run an event successfully then as long as they are still accountable and successful, that structure is fine. I have seen it work many times and most people who participate with informal committee structures seem to really enjoy the process and still get excellent results.

The Chairman of the committee is responsible for finding the best structure for meetings and that may take some discussion and experimenting.

<u>Committee Chairman Attributes</u>
When a person accepts the position of chairing a committee, they are accepting the role of leader. Leadership is a much researched area with many different ideas on the topic. Some experts think that leaders are born and others think that leaders are made. In my experience, very few people think of themselves as leaders. So what should you do if you accept the position as the committee chairman but you do not think of yourself as a leader? The way I see it, whether you think of yourself as a leader or not, you really are a leader. You need to believe that in the right circumstances we are all capable of being a leader, it's just a matter of finding the right circumstances.

If you are a parent then you are already a leader. If you have ever owned a business or managed an office then you are already a leader. If you have ever worked in customer service you are already a leader because the attributes are the same (we'll get to these soon). If you are a teacher or nurse then you are already a leader, and so on. Even if all you can do is shop, then you are still a leader as I'm sure you'd be able to lead me on a shopping trip as I have no skills in this area.

If you are not confident about your ability to lead, it is probably because you have not had the opportunity to develop leadership confidence. It is only through practising leadership that we can develop confidence at it. Unfortunately, the opportunity to lead is rarely available as established groups already have a leader and this denies other members the opportunity to gain leadership experience.

So how can you develop your leadership skills if you feel like you are not getting the opportunity to lead? One good way is to start with leading smaller groups for a while (e.g. a sub-committee), before progressing to the leadership of a whole committee.

Over the past twenty years I have worked closely with over 200 committees and some of those committees have been dismal failures, some have had mediocre results and some have been outstanding successes. It is indeed interesting to observe the attributes that the outstandingly successful committees have in common and what the dismal failures are missing. Interestingly, the most outstanding common feature of successful committees is that the chairman exhibits a few core attributes. If the chairman exhibits these few qualities then the committee will most likely achieve its goals, the members will be happy, and over time more people become interested in joining the group.

The three essential qualities a good chairman should possess are;

- Firmness—the chairman should be in control of meetings and the progress of tasks,
- Fairness—being impartial and reasonable, and
- Respect—the regular demonstration that other people are appreciated and valued.

Any person who chairs a committee and exhibits these three attributes will run a successful event and have a happy committee along the way. Chairmen who don't have all these qualities could either work towards achieving them, or share the leadership role with a vice-chairman, secretary or treasurer whose attributes would supplement and compliment theirs.

Some successful leaders also exhibit other attributes like drive, charisma, extroversion, etc, but I've found just as many successful leaders who do not exhibit any of these attributes. These attributes are great for a committee to have but it is not necessary for the chairman to have them. They can be bought to the committee very successfully by other members. You may well disagree with this point and insist that good leaders need to have these qualities, but I am reporting here what works in the real world.

Whilst all leaders bring a mixture of different attributes to the role of chairman, the key attributes that leaders need to run successful committees is to be firm, fair, and respectful of all members. I have even experienced chairmen who lacked self-confidence and were generally timid people, but because of their ample servings of firmness, fairness, and respect, they have been excellent leaders.

Let's look at these attributes in more detail.

Firmness
The chairman must be in control of the meeting and use that control to guide the committee to find decisions and outcomes which represent the group. The firmness of the chairman should be such that they follow the agreed meeting procedure closely without being too fanatical about it. Long gone are the days where volunteer members will sit in meetings and be fully cognisant of formal meeting procedures.

I have seen meetings where the chairman has been too strict and meetings where the chairman has been too relaxed for the circumstances. Both these extremes are bad for committees and produce inherently different outcomes. Too strict, and members will leave saying that they never get a chance to be heard. Too relaxed, and members will leave saying that the meeting went far too long and nothing was achieved.

Without going to extremes, there are still times for being firm or lenient. For example, if you are chairing a meeting when it becomes apparent that a member has failed to complete their task by the scheduled date, then you are now presented with two challenges;

1. get the task completed, and
2. ensure the member is not embarrassed or ridiculed.

Everybody has things that pop up in their lives from time to time that can distract them from their committee tasks. These distractions can often be very important like the health of a family member or the workload at their paid work increasing. No volunteer should ever be embarrassed publicly in a meeting for failing to complete their tasks. I've always adopted a process of rewarding the members who successfully complete their tasks on time with public recognition. This is quite a powerful tool as all the members will quickly come to understand your process and seek to be accepted and recognised. Those members who do not achieve their tasks will notice the absence of pubic recognition and quickly become aware of their failures but without public embarrassment. Extra effort can then be provided off-line to these members.

On the topic of being firm there is another matter which should be discussed. Some committees may experience disharmony between members. Most often this is a case of one member who is difficult to please upsetting other members. Some of the consequences of disharmony are that members will stop coming to meetings to avoid the confrontations or the meetings will get bogged down by tedious discussions to please the difficult member.

As the chairman you will have to resolve this problem before it gets to this point. This will be the true test of your firmness. Your actions here will be watched closely by all members to see how you can handle the situation.

On one committee that I chaired, the members of the committee included three people who were pedantic about small details which had little or nothing to do with the goals of the organisation. Previous meetings had been dominated by long discussions on irrelevant topics. These members had been allowed to control the discussions and the agenda from the floor.

Without being too strict, I firmly limited the discussion time allowed to these topics and within a few short months these people stopped coming to meetings. Had I confronted the irrelevant issues they were raising at meetings it would have led to a public showdown. Instead, all that needed doing was to limit the time these people had for their 'off topic' discussions and they consequently lost interest in coming to the meetings. Whilst I am disappointed that we lost three members they were more than replaced with new members once word got around that our meetings were now more effective, harmonious and shorter. All it took was one simple initiative firmly enforced.

Fairness
Being fair means being impartial and reasonable. This attribute is necessary during meetings and during other interactions with members.

Being able to treat members fairly will mean that you will have to forgo the natural tendency to consider that your opinion is more important than everyone else's. It is quite normal to believe that your opinion is somehow more correct than other people's opinions, but you will have to leave your opinions aside in order to be seen as a fair leader. It is simply not fair to force your opinions onto other people especially in a volunteer committee.

Being the chairman is not about being superior; you are just simply the person who guides the group towards making the decisions possible.

Being fair means listening to peoples suggestions, seriously considering what they are suggesting and then getting into a dialogue about the pro's and con's of the suggestion. To dismiss suggestion without full and open discussion will lead to alienation of members and more than likely the loss of some very good suggestions. I have seen many, many leaders who think that their opinion carries more weight than the opinion of an ordinary member and as such they tend to dismiss new suggestions that don't fit in with their 'Grand Plan'. These types of leaders will never be able to achieve as much as leaders who treat members fairly by seriously considering all reasonable suggestions.

Some experts believe there are three types of leadership styles; authoritative, participative and laissez-faire.

Authoritative leadership is where the leader makes decisions in isolation about what is good of the group.

Participative leadership is where the leader assists the group to make group decisions for the common good of the group.

Laissez-faire leadership is where the leader allows the individuals in the group to make their own individual decisions without guidance.

The Authoritative style works well in situations where high levels of risk are involved such as the Armed Forces and Police

Departments. This style is not advised when working with volunteer fundraising committees where physical risk is limited.

The Participative style works incredibly well where volunteers are involved but will also work well in most other organisations.

The Laissez-faire style has some limited uses in serious organisations however it should not be used in volunteer organisations.

In order to be fair as the chairman of your organisation, you will definitely want to be seen as a participative leader who assists the committee to make group decisions for the common good of the group.

Respect

Respect is the regular demonstration that other people are appreciated and valued. This should be demonstrated to all people but especially to volunteers on your committee. Volunteers are unique people who somehow find the time, energy and money to help support your cause. This alone makes them worthy of respect. However as not all people will be to your liking, this could sometimes become a hard task.

So how can you show respect for someone that you may not like but happens to be on your committee?

It is important for you to understand the difference between liking someone and respecting them. Next time that you are with a person that you don't like, try looking really hard at them to find out what drives them, what hardships they have in their life, how do they cope with them, what things may have happened to them in their life? I can usually find respect for someone, no matter how unhelpful, disruptive or manipulative they may be, once I understand they are just simply doing their best to achieve their personal goals as best as they can. They go about achieving their personal goals in a manner which they have learnt by personal experience over their lifetime. You are now a part of the influences in their life and you should strive to be a positive one and have a significant positive impact on them. If you can find a way to respect difficult people they will respond, often immediately, by becoming more harmonious.

I have worked on committees with many people that I didn't particularly like, but once I found a way of respecting them as an individual, I found that they became happier and more involved members. This generally leads to the entire committee being happier and functioning more smoothly.

If all this is new to you and you manage to get a good grasp on using firmness, fairness and respect, then not only will the committee function more successfully but you will have learnt some new skills that will help you in all aspects of your life.

<u>Making Decisions</u>
One of the responsibilities of the chairman is to get the informed opinion of the majority of the group accepted as an approved decision of the group.

Getting an *informed* opinion from a group of people is difficult at the best of times. People listen and learn in different ways and discussions on topics don't always clearly inform all people in the room. Some people may be listening emotively, others intellectually. Some may apply rational thinking to it and others irrational thinking. Getting an *informed* opinion from the group is very different from getting an agreed opinion.

Usually in committees, certain members would have responsibility for different aspects of an event and they would be required to report on their progress at the meetings. Sometimes these reports are very thorough and other times they may be quite brief. Regardless of its length, if a report is lacking in detail or seems to have a strangely biased viewpoint then the chairman needs to encourage a full and frank discussion about it. The chairman has the responsibility to ensure that a full unbiased discussion occurs on important issues even if they have to do the talking themselves.

I have chaired meetings where certain members wanted a particular outcome on a certain issue and when they discuss the issue they put forward only one point of view and they put it quite strongly. It is important not to let the committee make premature decisions based on only half the facts offered in a biased report. Therefore in this circumstance it is far better for you to offer some additional thoughts yourself just to ensure that when members make their votes, they are making an *informed* vote. If the discussion on the topic is completed and you still feel that the committee are not sufficiently informed to make a good decision, you should hold over the issue till the next meeting to provide additional opportunity for further consideration.

After all these years of chairing committees I still find that getting an *informed* vote one of the biggest challenges of being chairman. Informed votes are important because the real power of committees comes from the combined knowledge of all participants working together to form and achieve common goals. The common good of the group is thus enhanced as each individual participant provides their own particular skills to achieve group tasks.

One temptation to avoid is forcing your opinion onto the committee. This is one of the main pitfalls that a chairman must avoid. Often committee members will seem to be quite happy to just sit there quietly and let you do that, but I assure you they will be thinking to themselves how unfair you are being and you are likely to lose them as members if it continues.

As the chairman you will be immersed in the details of almost every issue that comes before the committee and thus you will develop a very strong knowledge on most issues. You must use this knowledge wisely and let the members bring their knowledge to the committee first. When you do this they will become more engaged and empowered and become better members as a result.

In fact when chairing committees I try to be known as a chairman without an opinion. Naturally I will always have a preferred outcome for each topic but I try not to voice this opinion in meetings. As the chairman, my role is not to get my opinion accepted, but to find the best decision from the group. To demonstrate the importance of the chairman not influencing discussions too much, on some committees the chairman does not even get a vote unless the vote of the ordinary members is deadlocked.

Once the committee makes a decision, that decision should become the accepted opinion of all of the people in the group especially the chairman. There is no place on volunteer committees for members who undermine committee decisions after they have been made.

If your committee has adopted a formal structure, making official decisions is made in a formal manner. There seems to be a few different methods used in Australia but here is the official way for it to happen at public meetings as described in 'The Australian Guide to Chairing Meetings' by Marjorie Puregger[3].

- Mover puts a motion
- Mover may speak for the motion
- Seconder seconds the motion
- Seconder may speak for the motion
- Chair reads the motion
- Discussions for & against the motion
- Mover has right of reply
- Chair again reads the motion
- Vote

For most volunteer fundraising committees this system is too cumbersome and unwieldy. Instead an abbreviated system something like this is commonly used;

- Discussion on a topic
- Chair calls for a motion
- Mover puts a motion
- Seconder seconds the motion
- Vote

However when I'm chairing a meeting, if I anticipate that the vote will not be unanimous (you can usually tell by the way the initial discussions went) I add a final discussion before the vote;

- Discussion on a topic
- Chair calls for a motion
- Mover puts a motion
- Seconder seconds the motion
- Final discussion for and against
- Vote

This system is simple and extremely fair as it gives everyone a chance (or two) to put their point of view.

Inclusive Communications
Wherever a volunteer committee exists there should be a culture of trying to minimize expenses. This sometimes leads to suggestions that to save money they should not distribute the minutes of the meetings but this is a bad idea. If a member misses a meeting or two and doesn't receive minutes then how are they to know what the group is up to? This lack of awareness about committee activities could make it embarrassing for them to return to future meetings and participate again. The last thing people want from joining a volunteer committee is to be publicly embarrassed.

The best way to keep all members feeling involved (even if they miss a few meetings) is to distribute minutes and newsletters to all members.

When a meeting date is set, this information should be sent to all members as soon as possible. Getting notification of a meeting a week before it's due to be held is just not enough notice for most people to be able to rearrange their schedule. If a committee member misses a few meetings then they can then get out of sync with the rest of the committee. One good way to ensure meeting dates are informed to all members is to have the next meeting details in large print at the end of the minutes which are distributed promptly after the each meeting.

Some organisations have an executive committee which runs the organisation and general members who are not on the executive. These general members also have a need to know what is going on amongst the executive committee although sending minutes to non-executive members is not always appropriate. The meeting minutes may contain sensitive information and it is not appropriate to distribute this information too widely. In this situation, I suggest that a regular newsletter also be produced and distributed to all members not just the executive. Newsletters are a wonderful way of distributing information about the committee's achievements, and sharing the committee's vision for the direction of the organisation in order to unite the whole organisation.

The newsletter needs to have a professional appearance and with the multitude of computer programs available this should not be a difficult task. There is often a member on the committee who has a special interest in computers who can achieve this. If not, it may be worth paying a professional to do it for you. The money may not be getting spent on your core business, but it will result in a more effective organisation and therefore more funds raised.

Meeting Times

One of the first orders of business for any new committee is to set meeting times. This can be quite a difficult task as it is common that only a few people will be available at any particular time. In fact it is better to have a meeting time in mind when recruiting new members so they will have the option of pulling out early if the meeting time doesn't suit them. However most people have some flexibility to rearrange their obligations to suit the meeting time if given enough notice.

Ensure the committee has an open discussion about suitable meeting times and that it decides on a preferred meeting time that suits most people. After that, if a member says that he or she is unable to attend at the preferred time then there is little that you can do about it and you may have to set that time anyway. That member may still be able to help with the event by taking on a lesser role as a sub-committee member who does not attend meetings. This is not a perfect solution but it does keep that person involved and it doesn't alienate them from the cause or the event.

When setting a meeting time you should have a realistic idea of how long the meetings will go for. Lunch and breakfast meetings are excellent for providing a mandatory deadline when members have to get back to work, but are prone to not finishing before the agenda is completed, or even worse running overtime and members being late back to work. Evening meetings are known for being more relaxed but also prone to going for longer with more difficulty keeping discussion on topic.

In the end the choice will be yours when setting a meeting time and it will always be a decision which requires the balancing of several different needs.

Chapter 4

Identifying The Benefits

When staging a fundraising event, the committee should be very clear about what benefits they seek from the event. With fundraising activities there is always more than one benefit possible. Other than raising funds, some of these benefits may be quite hidden at first but on closer inspection they do exist and are quite useful benefits to attain. Other benefits that can be achieved are;

- Services/resources that can be provided with the funds raised,
- Promotion of the organisation,
- Promotion of the cause,
- Attraction of prospective new members,
- Development of existing members, and
- Development of the event for future growth and income.

Often when a fundraising event is held, the primary goal for the event is to raise funds in the short term for provision of services and/or resources. However, all of the benefits of the event should be considered as important and worthy of consideration. Let's look at these in more detail;

Services/resources that can be provided by the funds raised.

When running a fundraising event you should have an idea of how much financial benefit you want to raise for the cause. You should know this figure before you work out how much the event could raise. This knowledge will help you with the decision of selecting an appropriate fundraising event. If the service or resources required by your cause costs $5,000, there is no point running a raffle which will raise only $500 (unless you plan on running ten of them).

Once you have selected an appropriate fundraising event, during the planning for it you must keep a steady focus on the objective of the services or resources which will be provided. This is often very difficult in the hectic rush of running a fundraising event with so many other tasks to think about, but I suggest that at each meeting a very brief discussion is held about the services or equipment sought.

If the fundraising event you are planning has not been run by your organisation before, predicting the amount of benefit in the way of funds raised can involve a lot of guesswork. Even applying standard financial practices to a first time event can be quite inaccurate as there are just so many unknown factors. Despite this you should still put a budget down on paper and get a few trusted friends to review it for you. This may provide a reasonable 'road map' for your event. As the planning progresses, keep updating the budget so that you always have a current 'road map' of where you are.

Promotion of the organisation.

In today's competitive world, it is likely that the cause for which you are raising funds is also a cause which attracts support from other organisations. For example, you may be raising funds for your child's soccer club and at the same time seeking to raise awareness of the club itself. In this example, the cause would be children's health and fitness whilst the organisation is the soccer club.

There are probably plenty of other soccer clubs promoting themselves in public at the same time you are, so it is very important that your particular club maintains it's profile within the marketplace. Raising the profile of your organisation is an important benefit of running a fundraising event.

If your organisation is to maintain long term viability in raising funds for the cause, the organisation must be recognised by the community as a worthy organisation. In order to achieve this, all promotional undertakings should feature the name and logo of the organisation displayed in a high quality manner.

If you run regular successful fundraising activities there will definitely be a benefit to the organisation with an increase in profile and respect in the community. The higher the profile of your organisation the greater good it can do for the community and the identified cause. In turn, if the organisation becomes very well known from previous successful fundraising activities, that strong profile can make current fundraising much more successful. This is a case of positive results feeding future growth.

Promotion of the cause.
Whenever an event is held in the public arena, one of the side benefits is that the public becomes more aware of the cause. This happens because the public promotion of the event should always mention and discuss the cause as well as the event. Public awareness of the cause could well flow through to more general support for your cause which can only help in resolving it.

People who attend one of your fundraising events have already shown a willingness to support your cause. Take the opportunity at the event of providing some further information to your supporters about how worthy your cause is. If you do this, the participants at your event will become better informed about your cause and may even become more regular supporters. You could do this by having a promotional display present, handing out brochures, or making speeches about the services your organisation provides.

Attract prospective new members.
Many community organisations consider that they are in need of more members. Running fundraising events with insufficient members can be very demanding and result in burning out the current members. In order to avoid burning out your current members, organisations need to have sufficient members to share the work among more people and therefore make lighter work for each person.

When people see your organisation out in the public running successful events and actually making a difference in the world by helping a needy cause, it is likely some people may feel inclined to want to join you. The old saying still is true; "Success breeds success". In order for success to breed success for you, your organisation has to be seen being successful. As people see your organisation successfully undertaking meaningful activities they will be open to the idea of joining with you to help build on your success.

This benefit can be developed and encouraged by having information about your organisation (including joining info) available at your event. As enquiries often come during a personal contact with current members, all of your members should be well trained about appropriate things to say during these initial enquiries.

As new people come along to join your committee and help organise fundraising activities, they should be made to feel not only welcome and useful but also as equals and friends. Working with volunteers is nothing like working with paid staff. Volunteers do not have an employee's commitment to tolerate hardships and thus they are more likely to leave if something goes wrong. To overcome this problem a committee should make volunteers feel equal and valued. This will encourage more loyalty from them and they will be more inclined to stay with the organisation.

One important additional thing that I try to always impress on committee members and volunteers at the start of planning for an event, is that we don't want to burn anyone out. Running a successful fundraising event has no long term gain if you lose members as a result. Saying this out loud at the start of planning can give the members confidence in you as the leader that you will care for their well-being.

Development of existing members.
The success of your organisation will not only be dependant on the quantity of your members but also on the quality. Do they have the skills required to run events successfully? Are they capable of working together well? Are they capable of focusing on the purpose and goals of your organisation?

If the answer to any of these questions is no, then something needs to be done to bring these qualities to the committee. There are two ways of bringing these qualities to your committee; training or experience. Both these techniques should be used where available however in many volunteer organisations training opportunities are pretty limited, so volunteers generally tend to develop their event planning skills through experience.

Whenever you run a successful fundraising event your members will naturally benefit from the learning experience. The individual tasks required to organise the event will require particular skills and as your members undertake these tasks they will become more proficient in them. Learning by doing is a very powerful tool and one which volunteers are particularly suited to use.

Most leaders would understand that the best way to get a task achieved is to give it to someone who has the necessary skills. This type of job assignment is very common and of course it works well. However sometimes you will need to consider the possibility of developing new skills in your members by challenging them in new skill areas. In the long term this will bring extra dimensions and a broader skill base to your members helping to provide a greater likelihood of being able to run more successful events in the future.

The benefit of developing your existing members is one which will have a long term positive effect on your organisation and your individual members.

Establish the event for future growth and income.
Not all fundraising activities make money in their first year. Many activities only become successful after years of establishing and growing the popularity of the event. Organisations run these events because they believe in the long term they will become financially successful. The future income of any event is not as valuable as current income in this year, but it can become more important if the event continues to grow.

Many fundraising activities are annual events and the public perception of your event this year will undoubtedly affect the success of the event next year. The initial impression of your event that people form at this year event will create a lasting impression on them. This impression will affect the likelihood of their attendance or support in future years. The benefit of future income needs to be protected, nurtured and encouraged by making this year's event a real winner.

There is one other situation to be cautious of. I've sat on many committees where imaginative people have come up with concepts for big new events that have the potential to generate big incomes. Many members will naturally feel that the big incomes will come in the first or second year of staging the event which is rarely if ever the case. In order to manage member's perspectives of this situation I have a little saying that I often use in these situations. That is; "All the successful big events in operation today, started small and grew big over a number of years". To establish an event as a big income producer it is almost always necessary to run it for a number of years whilst building the size of the event each year. If starting big events was easy then we would all be doing it.

If your committee chooses to establish an event for anticipated future growth and income, then this benefit may be more important than the benefit of raising funds for the current year. Even if current income is important to you the benefit of future income must still be considered.

SECTION 2

The Secret Key

Chapter 5

Identifying The Cause

Fundraising for a cause can be one of the most rewarding experiences that a person can have. It is an undertaking that many people undertake and reap significant benefits from, both for the organisation and for themselves personally.

Obviously the most significant issue with any fundraising activity is the 'cause'. By 'cause' I mean who or what will benefit from the fundraising. The popularity of cause can have huge impact on the success of your event.

The most important issue with the cause is; how much appeal does it have to the general public. If you want to get money out of people's pockets, the cause will need to be of significant relevance to them. The broader the appeal of your cause, the more likely people will be willing to support it. For example, when I was President of my children's school Parents & Citizens Association, running events that appealed to the parents of the school were very successful. Inviting people from the general public to these events had far less success because the cause (the quality of facilities at my children's school) had very little relevance to them. This cause had a very specific appeal to a very narrow group.

In short, people will support a cause that provides them, their family or their community with possible benefits. The more relevance a cause has to a person, the more likely they are support it.

This point becomes more obvious when you consider one of Australia's 'Blue Chip' causes; Surf Life Saving. Fund raising for Surf Life Saving Clubs is very effective in areas near the beach but further inland it receives less support from rural people. In these areas it must compete with other excellent causes which are of greater significance to rural people.

Other leading 'Blue Chip' charities like Cancer Council Australia enjoy significant levels of support evenly throughout all of the country. This is because the cause affects people everywhere throughout the country regardless of where they live. People are willing to help create a general benefit to their community because cancer affects most families in one way or another. This particular cause has real relevance to all families.

When deciding to stage a fundraising event you must first clearly identify the cause. Also during this stage it is important for the people involved on the committee to identify with the cause themselves. The general public will be unlikely to support events where the organisers themselves appear detached from the cause. In this situation, the event may take on the appearance of a commercial venture and therefore be less worthy of their philanthropic support. To ensure that the committee identify with cause, you may want to provide information to them about the hardships being endured by the community because of the cause.

If you feel that the general public will also be able to identify with the cause then you could consider running a fundraising event that aims to attract the general public. Otherwise it would be wise to only stage events that appeal to your own group of supporters.

Attracting the general public to a fundraising event has three powerful advantages;

1. You will be able to raise <u>more funds</u> than just fundraising internally in your group,
2. You are less likely to "burn out" the same small group of supporters, and
3. You will be <u>educating the broader community</u> about your cause and the need to support it.

There's no doubt that attracting the general public to your fundraising event can provide some significant benefits however there is also an incumbent risk with running events for the general public. If the general public cannot see real benefit to themselves, their family, or the general community, a public event is unlikely to attract much public support.

If your cause truly has limited appeal to the general public but you still wish to run a fundraiser designed to attract the general public, there is one strategy that can be used to broaden your event's appeal. By providing some of the profits from your event to a much more popular cause, you should be able to promote their cause in conjunction with yours and fundraise for both. Both charities win and the public will feel good supporting both causes. Having two causes as beneficiaries adds an extra dimension to the event planning but it can operate very smoothly if done properly. You will need to ensure that both organisations agree on all the critical aspects of the event (especially the promotion).

Some organisations, especially service organisations like Rotary, Lions, Apex, Zonta, Quota, etc., raise funds for distribution to charities. When service organisations fundraise, the general public still need to know the cause which will benefit from their donation before they would be willing to support it. Therefore promotion of fundraising activities which proudly announce their needy cause, are far more likely to experience success.

Chapter 6

Selecting The Fundraising Event

If you're reading this book it's probably because you're involved with a group that is either currently running fundraising activities or you're looking for a new activity to stage. Either way, you'll need to spend some time thinking about the vast array of fundraising activities available and then select one that suits your group.

I have worked with many very experienced fundraising committees in small towns and large cities alike, and one thing in common with them all is they experience considerable difficulty in finding new fundraising ideas that suit their town and committee. Often these committees have tried and exhausted all of the good ideas they could come up with and now they're currently scratching their heads trying to come up with a new idea for a fundraising event. Committees in this situation have stalled and need outside help to come up with something new that will suit their town and their committee.

When selecting a new fundraising event, committees should understand that each fundraising activity has unique aspects that can be used to define it. Understanding these different dimensions of fundraising activities is critical to helping you select an appropriate activity. The four important dimensions of fundraising activities are;

1. The profits that it can produce,
2. The time required for planning it,
3. The number of people required to organise it, and
4. The number of people required to stage it (the crew).

Each of these elements can be measured, and therefore each activity can be defined using these four dimensions. For example, a particular fundraising activity might have the following unique aspects that define it;

A Carwash

| Income **$50-$300** | Planning Time **3-10 weeks** | Committee **3** | Crew **10-20** |

Income
It is very rare for a Carwash to actually lose money or in fact make less than $50 income but they are generally limited to income under $300. It is quite possible to make more than $300 but this would be an unusually good result.

Planning Time
You could organise one in 3 weeks or if you wanted more time it could be as far away as 10 weeks but it is quite unusual for planning times outside of this time frame.

Committee
A committee of about 3 is a good number.

Crew
On the day you would need between 10 and 20 people to make it a success.

In Appendix 1 there is a comprehensive list of fundraising activities complete with estimations of each dimension for that event. You can use this list to make the task of selecting your next fundraising activity an easier one. The list is quite extensive and accounts for the majority of fundraising events in use today. It has information on hundreds of great ideas which will put you in the driver's seat when selecting your next fundraising activity.

The dimension listed in Appendix 1 can be used to help you decide whether the activity is one that matches the resources of your group and the income that you seek. They show what can be achieved in normal circumstances. Of course there are organisations in Australia that could stage these activities more or less successfully and in some cases this can be significantly more or less successfully. The figures shown in Appendix 1 are provided as a guide of average results to assist in the comparison of the various activities.

Appendix 1 is a guide that will help you and your committee select an activity to run which matches the resources of your group and the funds that you wish to raise. When selecting an activity it is of uppermost importance that you have, or can get, the resources shown, i.e.;

- The planning time,
- The committee, and
- The crew.

Obviously these three dimensions are not the only ones required to stage successful fundraising activities, but if these three core resources exist the other resources can usually be located. These three core resources are the ones which have the greatest impact on the success of fundraising activities.

In Appendix 1 the activities have been grouped into four different types for ease of selection. They are;

- Sell Something,
- Run An Event,

- Run A Business, and
- Ask For Help

It is certainly worth a good long look at all the activities in these groups as you may be surprised at which groups and activities would be suitable for your committee.

In each group some activities are quite simple and easy to manage and others are huge tasks requiring very established and experienced organisers. Please pay attention to the resources required before deciding if an activity suits your group.

It is a common feature of most fundraising activities that they have the potential to be large demanding endeavours or they could also be smaller, easier endeavours. For example a chocolate drive that is run by a scout group of 20 children will require substantially less resources than a chocolate drive which is run at a school with 1,000 children. A lot will depend on your ability to attract the participants to your activity.

That sure is a lot to keep in mind as you research the list for your next activity but there is also one more aspect to keep in mind if you want your activity to be successful. The activity has to be fun as well. If you take the fun out of fundraising then your crew of helpers and your participants will not be very interested in getting involved again next year and they may even lose interest in supporting your cause all together.

There is not much use putting in all the required hard work and long hours to establish your fundraising activity and make it successful if the activity does not go on to become an annual one. The reason for this is that all events and activities require more time and effort in their first few years to get established. Over time the committee will become more familiar with the event and learn the quickest and easiest way to get it done. The income is usually lesser in the early years and will increase in time also. So the benefits of a fundraising event become greater and the effort becomes less the longer an event runs which makes annual events very attractive.

Appendix 1 is a very comprehensive list of fundraising events although it does not include every activity possible. Fundraising is an exciting and quick moving industry which often attracts creative people with a natural tendency to develop new events or develop new twists to old events. Consequently the fundraising activities list can also be used as an aid to create or adapt new fundraising events.

So go ahead and select an activity from the fundraising activity list which matches the resources your group has and the income you seek to raise. You can then plan for it to be fun and successful in both the short and long term.

Chapter 7

Defining The Target Audience

Before we get into this chapter, the word 'audience' needs to be defined. In this book the word 'audience' is used to signify the people who support a fundraising activity in any way and there are generally three ways that the public can help. They may either donate, buy or attend. Officially these people would be called your customers, clients or your market. However with fundraising events, the word 'audience' best describes the involvement of the general public regardless of whether they donate, attend or buy.

Just as each fundraising activity has aspects that define it, so to does your target audience. Understanding your target audience is necessary in order to market your event to them. Marketing is a fascinating subject which impacts on everybody's life whether they know it or not. It has many definitions but most of them are similar to this one from The Cambridge Dictionaries Online[4]; *"to make goods available to buyers in a planned way which encourages people to buy more of them, for example by advertising"*.

In order to effectively market your event to the correct target audience, your committee will need access to some sound marketing advice. This advice commonly comes to committees from one of three main areas;

- Within the Committee—There is a growing reliance by committees on finding their marketing advice from people within their committee. All sort of people have a certain level of marketing knowledge now days, from small business owners, to government employees, to uni students and others. These people often have a remarkably savvy knowledge about marketing and can provide real value to the committee.

- Sponsor Support—To get professional marketing advice from an external source, some committees approach large local businesses with a request to sponsor their event by providing the use of their marketing professionals. Large businesses are now more willing to provide this type of 'in-kind' support which they are more comfortable with than providing direct monetary support.
- Beneficiary Support—Check with the organisation that you're raising funds for. Often they have marketing professionals who can provide free assistance to your committee as well.

In the end it doesn't really matter where the advice comes from as long as the committee has access to sound marketing advice that assists in defining who the target audience is for your event and helps you to promote it to them

Defining your target audience is not always difficult for fundraising events. If the event is only going to be marketed internally within your group, then the target market can be very easily defined. For example if you choose to do a chocolate drive within your school, then the target market are the children within the school, their parents, friends and neighbours. Easy!

Any event where the target audience is internal within your organisation, will be much easier to promote and far more likely to achieve its goals. However if you are seeking to run a large fundraising event which will attract the general public, you will need to understand <u>who</u> is likely to attend your event and also

<u>where</u> you can best direct your promotional activities to appeal to these people.

Let's look at a few examples;

Art Auction

Who   People who can afford to buy art—professional people, wealthy people.

Where   Industry newsletters, large businesses like hospitals, schools, government departments, lawyer firms, affluent suburbs.

Car Wash

Who   People with dirty cars—car owners.

Where   Busy roads and shopping centres.

Fun Run

Who   People who like to exercise—healthy, fit people.

Where   Running clubs, gymnasiums, High Schools.

Ambassadorial Quest

Who   People who aspire to modelling careers—girls 14 to 25.

Where   Modelling schools, dance schools, youth groups.

Raffles

Who   People who like to win things—all adults.

Where   Any place adults congregate, shopping centres, sporting venues, pubs & clubs, workplaces.

Car Rally

Who   People with an interest in cars—mechanically minded men.

Where   4wd clubs, pubs, sporting clubs, car racing venues, men's clubs.

I hope by now you will be able to see that no matter who your target audience is there are always places where your promotion will have a better chance of being noticed by them. It is just a matter of clearly defining who your target audience is and then considering where these people tend to gather.

Chapter 8

The ONE Secret Key to Fundraising Success

Events are very complex things to organise. There is the committee to consider, the event, and the audience. There are literally hundreds of details to organise for a fundraising event; so many in fact that it is very easy to become unfocused and confused about what aspects are the most important in making the event a success.

So how can event organisers identify what is the most important aspect of their event? Is there a simple formula for the success of fundraising activities?

Well the good news is, there is a secret key to attracting your target audience and it is a very simple one. You won't need seven keys, five keys, three keys or even just two keys. There is just one key to getting your target audience to support your fundraising event.

It is as simple as this;

Both the CAUSE _and_ the EVENT must be important to the AUDIENCE.

When planning a fundraising event, don't just think that because the cause is important people will want to support it, they largely won't. The event has to be highly valued by them as well.

Likewise, don't think that the event you are organising is highly valued to your target audience so people will want to come, they largely won't. The cause has to be important to them as well.

For example, if you are walking along the main street of your local shopping district and come across a sausage sizzle stall being run by a national health organisation, you are more likely to buy the sausage if you consider both sausages *and* the national health organisation as important.

Of course as an event organiser, you will still need the hundreds of other details to be arranged correctly. Just some that spring to mind for this particular example are; sausages, bread, onion, money float, volunteers, roster, training, tables, barbecue, drinks, eskies, cooking utensils, paper towel, signage, council approval, public liability insurance, volunteer insurance, worker compensation policy, etc. But given that these details are capable of being arranged by a competent committee, the key to getting the target audience to support your event is ensuring that both the cause *and* the event are important to them.

One example which demonstrates this is a committee of young women who were professional women and wives of professional men. They decided that they wanted to run a fundraising event to help raise funds for a local needy organisation. On their first meeting together they decided that they would run a Ball because they all enjoyed going to Balls and that "Balls are usually good fundraisers".

They planned the meeting times and places, the event date and venue, and then they got on with the planning for all of those hundreds of details which go into an event.

They identified two target audiences for the event, one was their friends and the other was people from the general public. They promoted the Ball to their friends by developing a very unique flyer and sending it directly to them through the mail. They promoted the Ball to the general public by using radio advertising and give-aways. They hoped that 100 people would come, with about half being friends and half from the general public. To their credit the committee worked very hard and did a lot of creative thinking with the event and its marketing.

When the night of the Ball came only about 60 people showed up at the event, but the interesting result was that only one person came from the general public and he came because he had won a free ticket on a radio station promotion. The night was actually a lot of fun but it made only a fraction of the profit it was hoped it would make. This was due to the great support the event received from the committee members friends but it did not achieve the level of financial success that the committee had hoped for due to the lack of attendance by the general public.

In other words, the event attracted only one of its target audiences but not the other. The general public did not see the Ball _and_ the cause involved as sufficiently important to them. The cause involved had a very broad appeal in the town but the event was not important to the general public. Attending a Ball is high effort activity and people who like to attend Balls probably already attend enough Balls each year. The effort and expense involved with attending a Ball is extensive with couples needing to organise suits and gowns, transport, reschedule other appointments, baby sitters, friends to attend with, etc. The costs to attend would start at $200 and could go up from there. A ball is a high effort and high cost event for your audience to consider attending.

So it turned out that the high effort and high cost involved with attending this event made the event not important enough for the general public to attend despite the cause being very worthy.

This secret key works for all fundraising events, but it is more important for some fundraising activities than others. For example a target audience would find it much easier to support a Sausage Sizzle than a Ball. The Sausage Sizzle takes just two minutes and costs $2 whereas the ball takes at least four hours and costs more than $200 to attend.

This leads to an important condition for the secret key. It is; **The more effort and cost involved for the target audience to support a fundraising event, the more important this secret key is.**

This condition for the secret key is quite useful to understand as it leads to a clever idea. If you are ever stuck with a cause that is not all that important to the target audience, then you should consider organising an event which does not require much effort or cost for the target audience to support. Perhaps you could choose to do a Shopping Centre Stall instead of a Ball. For the same amount of work, you could well achieve a much better financial result.

A good example of this is a scout group which was selling $2 raffle tickets in a Shopping Centre to buy some new equipment for their group. The cause had very little personal relevance for the shoppers and the prize was not all that attractive, but the raffle seemed to be going very well because the effort and cost involved for the target audience to support the event was very low.

To summarise;

The secret key of fundraising events is that both the CAUSE _and_ the EVENT must be important to the TARGET AUDIENCE.

The more effort and cost involved for the target audience to support a fundraising event, the more important this secret key is.

SECTION 3

The Event

Chapter 9

Event Planning

There's a saying in the Australian Army that goes; "There's nothing like a massive chest wound to remind you that your bushcraft skills are not up to standard." In its rather macabre way, this saying very simply says that there are dire consequences of poor planning for soldiers during battle. I'm very pleased to say that the consequences of poor planning for volunteer fundraisers are usually not as severe as they are for soldiers.

However the consequences of poor planning for a fundraising event are not something that any organiser wants to contemplate. No event that has been poorly planned has any chance of success and there are a thousand ways that an event can go wrong and unfortunately there are only a very few ways that it can go right.

When a volunteer fundraising event does turn out to be less successful than the organisers would have hoped, it is often because something was wrong in the planning. In most cases though, it is just one or two elements of the event that were not quite right but this can still spell disaster for the event.

At an Art Auction I attended once, the room was full and everyone was having a great time but the event failed to make much money. This was because very little art was actually sold. This of course was a huge disappointment for the organisers, the sponsors, the guests and the beneficiary organisation.

As I sat at the table with other guests, the conversation quickly turned to "Why is none of the art selling? As it turned out the wrong type of people attended the event; i.e. the target audience was not achieved! The organisers needed wealthy people who had the financial flexibility to purchase art to attend the function but this type of people did not attend. The people who came to the event were largely friends and family of the artists, many of whom already owned art from these painters.

The problem was a planning error as the committee had correctly identified its target audience but they had no formal promotional plan to attract this particular group.

In order to avoid this kind of disappointment and provide proper event planning there are essentially four documents that need to be produced. They are the;

1. budget,
2. work schedule,
3. promotional plan, and a
4. running sheet.

Sometimes a fifth document is prepared as well which shows the resources that are required for the event but this should only be needed for larger events which would usually have a paid staff member taking responsibility for this.

Let's look at the four main documents required in detail.

1. Preparing the Budget
When planning an event the first item to be prepared is the budget. The reason for this is the events financial success needs to be gauged before you become too emotionally attached to the event. If all the other planning is prepared first before the budget is done, and then the budget shows that making a profit would be a real challenge, some organisers may choose to proceed with

the event anyway as they have already invested so much time and effort into it. This is the wrong way to do an event and emotions should not be a part of the decision making process.

Even the best budget is only as good as the ability of the committee to foresee all of the costs and to accurately estimate the potential income. Once the budget is finished and everyone is happy with it, it is smart to encourage committees to think of the budget as the best case scenario. In practice it is very, very rare for additional income to come along above the budgeted amount, but unfortunately it is very, very common for additional unforeseen and unexpected expenses to appear from nowhere.

In subsequent years of an annual event the budget will become much firmer and more predictable and the effort required to achieve it will be significantly reduced.

A copy of a good budget layout to use is in Appendix 2 for use as a guide.

2. Managing the Work Schedule

The second item to prepare is a work schedule. If you don't prepare a written work schedule people will either sit around wondering what to do or want to head off in their own directions. At this stage it is imperative to have a talk about work schedules. I know that nobody likes work schedules least of all volunteers, but when people give their valuable time to help a good cause raise some much needed funds, they don't like to see their time wasted. Work schedules are the only way to achieve this.

A work schedule for a small event (for example with only two or three people organising it), can be a simple verbal discussion about what each person will do and when. A more complex work schedule than this is would be over-planning and wasteful in itself for such a small event.

However once you start planning for anything other than a very small event, a written work schedule should be prepared. There are a few different ways that work schedules can be prepared and they all work well in certain circumstances and for certain people. I'm going to tell you about three methods that I use, the Promotional Flyer method, the 'To Do' List method, and the Gantt Report method. For very big events you may want to consider using one of the computer programs that are available for project management like Microsoft Project® however I won't be discussing them here as this book is for volunteer fundraisers and these programs are most commonly used by professional fundraisers running very large events.

Promo Flyer
This style of work schedule is suitable for small committees undertaking small activities. The first thing to do is start developing a Promotional Flyer that would be used to promote the event. To complete this flyer you will have to know such information as;
Name of the Event
Day and Date
Times
Venue
Entry Fee
Activities
Motivation/Drawcard
Who you're Targeting

In order to determine all of these details, the committee will have to make decisions about them. In order to make these decisions, the committee will first have to undertake many of the tasks required i.e. the date and time can't be confirmed until the venue is booked. The process of confirming the details for the Promotional Flyer completes the planning for a smallish event.

It is a back to front way of organising an event, but for smaller activities with smaller committees it is a very easy way to identify what needs doing and gets you started doing it.

An example of a Promotional Flyer is in Appendix 3.

'To Do' Lists

To Do lists are the next step on from the Promo Flyer. Instead of just letting the committee members go off and organise the tasks they are responsible for, the whole process is written down and put into a spread sheet. The spread sheet contains a complete list of ALL the individual tasks required to be done listed down in the first column. They are grouped into categories of their relevant areas. For example, if you were running a school fete the categories may be;

Class Stalls
Student Displays
Stage Entertainment
Catering
Promotion
General

Each one of these categories will have a number of tasks that need to be completed and each category would have a committee member responsible for it. These committee members may well also have a subcommittee to assist with the portfolio.

The headings across the top of the table are:

Column 1—The task
Column 2—Who is responsible for each task
Column 3—When it needs to be completed by
Column 4—Comments

When allocating tasks to committee members it is not effective to put a person's name on the spread sheet if they are not willing or interested in doing the task. You will need to ensure that all people who agree to undertake a task, understand what is required and personally accept responsibility to complete it by the due date.

The 'To Do' list is updated with the latest information from the committee members at each meeting and reprinted prior to the next meeting. Volunteers are usually very comfortable with the 'To Do' list as an acceptable form of work schedule. It is not a complicated form like Gantt Reports and it is not a loose control like the Promotional Flyer style. If the tasks that have been completed are shaded a different colour to those tasks that are yet to be completed, then it is very easy to see at a glance which tasks are still current and therefore require discussion at the meetings. Coloured 'to Do' lists are therefore very useful for focusing the committee on the important tasks yet to be completed, and they can also be used as a thorough agenda for committee meetings.

'To Do' lists are the most common style of work schedules used by volunteer committees. They are well accepted, easy to prepare, easy to understand, and very thorough. For anything larger than a Car Wash and smaller than an Expo then I suggest the use of a 'To Do' list.

An example of a 'To Do' list is in Appendix 4.

GANTT Reports
GANTT Reports are the next step up from 'To Do' lists. They consist of a table that has the same information in the first two columns as the 'To Do' lists, but then there are additional columns with headings which are labelled as a calendar of dates leading up to the event. The body of the table contains indications of when each individual task needs to be started and completed. The GANTT Report is usually fully completed as the first item of event planning and it becomes the roadmap and timetable for

when each task is due to start and when it needs to be completed by. This report enables a visual indication of the expected progress of the entire event.

The GANTT Report is a great way to keep a large event on schedule. Without an indication of when certain tasks are required to be started and finished by, committee members may take away different interpretations of how urgent their particular tasks are. The GANTT Report shows all members how urgent each individual tasks is and importantly how other tasks are dependent on previous tasks being completed in a timely manner.

Even though the GANTT Report is a great way of tracking the progress of very complex events, they are not used for every large event. The problem with GANTT Reports is that they are very complex documents and volunteer committees often shun complexity in planning. With complex documents like Gantt Reports, volunteers can think that the event has become task oriented instead of people oriented and this can alienate some people.

Instead, sometimes the event leader could prepare a GANTT Report for their own personal use and keep it updated, but not show it to the committee. They could personally refer to it in meetings so they are acutely aware of the committee's progress, and then verbally discuss the progress with committee members. This 'non-public' GANTT Report works well for professional fundraisers who work with volunteer committees and are therefore charged with an over-arching responsibility to ensure the event is professionally managed.

An example of a GANTT Report is in Appendix 5.

3. Planning The Promotion
A promotional plan does not have to be a complex document. It contains a list of promotional activities planned, when they will

occur, what focus they will have and what media they will use. The important aspect of a promotional plan is that all promotions are directed towards attracting the attention, interest and action of the identified Target Audience.

Remember the story about the Art Auction which sold very little art. The event was promoted almost exclusively to family and friends of the artists when they really needed to attract a different audience of affluent people who appreciate art. Had a promotional plan been produced, it most certainly would have shown that affluent people with an appreciation for art read certain magazines and newspapers, shop in certain shops, and listen to certain radio stations. The promotional activities could then have been focused towards those media outlets.

A copy of a promotional plan is in Appendix 6.

4.   Producing a Run Sheet

The fourth item to prepare is a Run Sheet. This document is the program of events for the people involved with running the actual event. It will contain much more information than a program of events that you would receive if you were a guest at an event.

The entire committee should have a copy of the Run Sheet so that they can coordinate behind the scenes for the various activities. The Run Sheet should be completed and distributed at least a week before the event. This gives everyone a chance to become familiar with the timings and how they will need to fit in with them.

At events where an MC is being used, the MC will definitely require a copy of the committee's detailed Run Sheet. The MC is the person who stands in front of the audience and they announce the starting and stopping of the various activities scheduled. They will need a good understanding of the Run Sheet if they are to appear calm and confident in front of the audience.

I attended a fundraising event once where a committee had organised a gala dinner with 150 guests. The committee organised an MC for the night but did not think to produce a Run Sheet. Under the circumstances the MC did a fantastic job, but when it came time to introduce speakers he was unsure who to invite to the stage. He looked very foolish standing in front of 150 people asking committee members "Who's going to speak next?" On top of this there was no list of sponsors and supporters to thank, and as a result some important supporters were overlooked.

Believe it or not, Run Sheets are often overlooked in the haste of putting an event together. The event organisers have such a sound knowledge of the event they can easily forget that other key people do not. Having a Run Sheet will ensure that everything happens correctly on the night and that it all happens on time.

A copy of a Run Sheet is in Appendix 7 for use as a guide.

Chapter 10

Uncontrollable Occurrences

Unfortunately even with the best planning, sometimes a fundraising event can be the victim of an uncontrollable occurrence. If it rains during your outdoor event it can significantly affect the chance of financial success. Whilst rain is certainly an uncontrollable occurrence, some people think of rain as bad luck. They think that if it rains during their outdoor event, then they have been unlucky!

Have you ever heard the saying "The harder I work, the luckier I get"? This concept points to the fact that luck may completely fabricated. If you can become luckier with hard work then what is luck really anyway? Let's just forget about luck for a moment and investigate what chance is.

Chance is the measurable likelihood that a particular occurrence will happen, e.g. rain on a particular day. At any given time there is a certain chance of rain, it maybe 20:1 right now or it may be 200:1, but there is a definable chance. The chance of rain can be calculated and it is higher on some days than others.

It may be that managing chance is the key to success. By measuring the chance of an uncontrollable occurrence, we can plan to minimise its likelihood of occurring and minimizing its impact if it does occur.

There are too many uncontrollable occurrences that could impact on your fundraiser to discuss them all here. However we will discuss four such uncontrollable events here to demonstrate the concept and you can then apply the concept to your events. They are:

o   Poor Weather
o   Cancellation of Performers
o   Illness of Organisers
o   Unforeseen Conflicting Event

Whilst these occurrences appear to be uncontrollable, with a little forethought you should be able to make them less disastrous.

Poor Weather
If staging an outdoor event, choose a time of the year when poor weather is less likely. Where I live in Queensland, the rain usually comes as an afternoon thunderstorm during summer. Planning an event outside of these times will dramatically decrease the chance of poor weather.

If an event absolutely has to be held at a time of the year when poor weather is common, consider moving it to an indoor venue.

Some committees which stage outdoor events may consider taking out insurance for inclement weather and in fact one committee that I served on actually did take out such insurance. The event was a school fete and the insurance policy stipulated substantial rain had to occur over a substantial time period, not just drizzle or a shower. This was quite a rare event in our area, and spending money on this policy turned out to be a waste of money as it did not rain that year. However one other year it did rain on the fete and we made just as much money as other years because the fete ran for five hours and it only rained for half an hour. Having insurance for events with a turnover less than $50,000 is hard to justify.

One major outdoor event in the town where I live has been staged at lunchtime on the same Saturday every year for over fifty years. During this time it has experienced rain only once. This is largely due to the fact that lunchtime rain is very rare in Toowoomba in September which is when this event is held. See the chart below which shows that September is one of the lowest rainfall months of the year in my town.

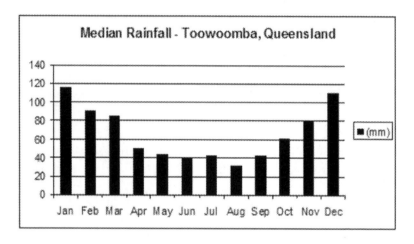

Figures are provided by The Australian Bureau of Meteorology[5].

There are no rainfall charts available that I am aware of that show the time of the day that rain is most likely to occur, but local knowledge can surely be of some guidance here.

So when considering the risk of poor weather, keep in mind that the real risk is probably less than you would think and that you can minimise the risk by staging the event during times of the year and times of the day and in certain locations when poor weather is less likely. If your event has a high profit level, insurance may be worth considering.

Cancellation of Performers

One of the most disappointing events that I have been involved with was an expo which was targeted at kids and their parents. In its second year, the organising committee decided to try to increase patronage by booking a major national drawcard at considerable expense to the committee. Six months before the event we booked two very popular and famous personalities from a successful Australian TV show. They were very popular with kids and were widely idolised. Not long after we signed a contract with the actors, the popularity of their show quickly declined and it was cut from TV just a month before our event. The event went ahead with the actors still appearing but the drawcard value of having them at the event was significantly reduced. That event failed to make a profit that year due to the additional cost of paying for celebrities without a corresponding increase in income.

The lesson to learn here is that incurring a large non-essential cost like paying for celebrities should be done very conservatively.

Whilst the failure of the celebrities to be a major drawcard does seem to be an uncontrollable event, there were things that we could have done to lessen the impact of this situation. Firstly we could have had two drawcards from different shows instead of two from the same show. That would have halved the effect if one them subsequently failed to be a drawcard. Secondly we could have decided to grow the event more slowly and wait until the event was producing enough income to carry the loss of the performer's fees.

There are other options that can minimise the impact of this uncontrollable event, but each situation will have its own solutions and your solutions will have to be found by you. Plan ahead for this uncontrollable event and have contingency plans ready. Often 'Plan B' works out better than 'Plan A' anyway.

Illness of Organisers

Ironically, as I write this section I am home sick having three days off work from my job as a professional fundraiser. It is now just two days before a major event and I have lost three complete days away from the preparations in the last week before the event.

As dreadful as that sounds, this year's event is truly on track for being the most successful yet.

The success of this year's event will be due largely to the way our committee works. Whilst I may be paid as the fundraiser, the event has a volunteer committee which has complete control over the event. Losing one person to illness at this stage just means that some of the other committee members take on a little more. So illness of any of the key organisers does not have to be detrimental to the event as long as there is a committee with the skills to share workloads around.

But what if you're in charge of an event and there are no supporters who can take over from you? Well you're in trouble and I recommend that you never put yourself in the position of being indispensable. Ensuring there is a supporting committee to help you with the event and genuinely sharing the knowledge of the event with them, is a key ingredient to success. Have thorough planning documents ready so that anyone can pick up from where you are up to in the event you become unavailable in the lead up to an event.

Similarly, if your committee has any people on it who are the only ones with knowledge about their portfolios, then the event is at serious risk if any of these members are suddenly unavailable. I recommend that you form subcommittees for each portfolio where all the tasks are shared amongst the subcommittee members. If there are not enough people to have subcommittees then consider having two people share two or three portfolios together. That ensures that there will never be a situation where the event relies on the attendance of any one key person.

When put into a position of responsibility for a fundraising event, your first responsibility is to do the job well but your second responsibility is to ensure that your first responsibility will be taken care of even you can't. That way your responsibilities will always be taken care of.

<u>Conflicting Event</u>
When setting a date for an event, most organisers are aware that they should find a date which does not conflict with other events in their area which would compete for the same Target Audience. The problem is that it is often very hard to find a calendar of events which lists all of the competing events. Most towns and regions have events calendars but it is rare to find one which is complete with all of the events in your region. Often there are multiple calendars in each region, each with different events listed on them.

Of all the uncontrollable occurrences, this one is the one that you can do the most to avoid. Search for calendars of events from your local area by asking at your local council, sporting bodies, tourism groups, service clubs, race clubs, etc. Get onto a search engine on the internet and search for the date that you are considering in your area and then broaden the search to your state and even the country. Keep in mind that a national football grand final in another state could well signal the doom for your local event if they are on at the same time.

State and Federal government election dates are commonly only announced 6 to 10 weeks in advance. If you set the date for your event six months in advance there's little you can do if an election is later called on the same day. Elections do have a way of changing people's recreation plans for the day and it will almost certainly have an impact on your event. If this uncontrollable occurrence happens and it's too late to change the date then look for a way to turn it into a positive. You could use the fact that everyone will be voting that day as an easy way to promote your event by having promotional signage on the streets around your area. As people are travelling to the polling booths they will be reminded about your event and as they are already out and about, they may well add your event to their activities for the day. Also, you could consider re-theming your event to have the flavour of the election and that may appeal to your target audience on the day.

If there is a conflicting event which you think will significantly affect your patronage and you can't do anything about it, identify this as early as possible and plan for a smaller event. Annual events commonly suffer a year where a decrease in patronage occurs. If you plan for it by reducing expenses accordingly then it will not be the death knell that it could have been. Then, in future years you will be able to continue growing the event.

Chapter 11

Supervision

If there is one place where most volunteer fundraising events fall down, it is in the supervision of the volunteers. Volunteers who take on leadership roles within a volunteer committee can often be reluctant to supervise other volunteers. This is most likely because they feel that;

a) they are not very good supervisors, or
b) it won't be appreciated by the volunteer.

Whilst volunteers are a unique breed of people and they often bring high levels of motivation with them, they will still require a leader to guide them through the planning stages of an event. Undertaking a leadership role infers that you will be largely responsible for the success of the event. As the leader of a volunteer fundraising committee, you are required to ensure that committee members achieve their agreed tasks.

Remember from chapter 3 that good leaders always demonstrate firmness, fairness and respect.

One common occurrence that can occur with volunteer committees is when a committee member starts missing committee meetings. This leaves the rest of the committee without any progress report for that portfolio and wondering if the tasks have been done or not. If this situation is left unchecked the committee will start to assume the tasks have not been done and therefore become concerned the overall success of the event is being threatened.

The leader really needs to resolve this problem before it is left to go on for to long. The wayward committee member absolutely must be contacted and their progress ascertained. It is preferable to do this before a committee meeting if they have missed more than one, so that a new course of action can be discussed at the meeting and not postponed for another month.

In the difficult situation where a committee member has not come to meetings and is not available to be contacted, the committee needs to discuss what options are available that will ensure the tasks still get done. It is not a good idea to reallocate the tasks to another member until the committee leader has spoken directly with the wayward member. The reason for this is the wayward member may very well have achieved their tasks and been too busy to report back to the committee. If this happens you will totally alienate that member, annoy the member who was reassigned their tasks and have to go back and cancel the plans that the second member has made. Therefore you must accept the responsibility to contact the first member and ascertain their progress before their tasks are re-assigned.

If it eventually turns out that they have not undertaken their tasks, some leaders may now be tempted to replace them on the committee and reassign their tasks. This could still be a poor course of action as that member would be very embarrassed in front of the committee and you may loose a good volunteer who was temporarily distracted with another very important aspect of their life.

Instead, it is smarter to ask their permission to make their portfolio of tasks into a sub-committee, and then move some other volunteers in to help on this sub-committee. This way they are still empowered to help with the tasks when and if they are fully available again.

Other member will be watching how you handle this situation and it will set the tone for all members on the committee. If they see that you really value the efforts of all volunteers when and how they are able to help, the other volunteers will become more enthused to help and will make a greater commitment. If they see you cut a volunteer away from the committee for any reason, it is natural they will become unsure as to their own security on the committee and may become stressed about their continuing role on it. Remember that volunteers should always be made welcome no matter what their level of involvement. At some point in the future their other commitments may lessen and they could become more highly engaged with your committee.

Of course, throughout the supervision of this situation, you as leader need to ensure that the deadlines for the planning of the event are still being met. This may mean undertaking some of these tasks yourself until the wayward committee member is back on track. Volunteers really respect leaders who can demonstrate a willingness to get involved on any level so there is an upside to taking on the extra tasks yourself. However you must watch the tendency of personally taking on all the tasks that are not getting done on time. You can also share some of them around the committee in a fair and equitable way.

Supervision of the committee on the day of the event is another thing all together. During the lead up to an event decisions are generally made by the committee after significant discussions on each task. However once an event begins there is often no time for committee decisions and therefore decisions need to be made using a different decision making system. The best system for making decisions at an event is to provide each committee member with full responsibility for their portfolios whilst ensuring they provide regular updates to you on their progress and issues.

As the leader of the committee it is likely that you will be the only person who knows all the facets of the event and you will be highly in demand on the day. As the key person at the event, people will be coming to you throughout the event seeking information and guidance. This can be a demanding role as there is only one of you and multiple simultaneous demands on your time and knowledge can be very tiring.

The events that I have enjoyed running the most as the key person are the one's where I've had a co-coordinator. Having two lead coordinators will provide two people to share the workload during those multiple demand moments. Good co-coordinators will be equally involved with the planning of the event and know everything that is going on so that they are able to share the workload between them.

If you can't arrange a co-coordinator then having a 'personal assistant' will really help with the demanding times during the event. This is another way to ensure that everything gets done properly on the day without being too demanding on any single person.

Chapter 12

Celebrating The Results

So the event has been run and everything went well. There are typically a few things which will happen after an event;

1. You and your committee will be tired and emotional (either up or down). You could well have a significant 'low' two days after the event, this is normal even for successful events.
2. There is a list of 'loose ends' which need tidying up and there is no-one around to do them.
3. You will notice the other parts of your life which have been ignored during the exhilaration of the event and they will definitely be in need of attention.

Different people will handle these situations in their own ways with varying results. Some event leaders will completely leave an event the day it finished and go back to their normal life. Other event leaders may be so depressed after an event they need to rest for a week before they can do anything again. While other event leaders may well stay on a 'high' for a number of weeks afterwards.

Whatever the response you have to the completion of the event it is important for the committee to celebrate the results. The committee members have set their goals and worked hard to achieve them, they deserve a celebration. Here are a few ideas for how you could celebrate the success.

Directly after the event pack up, you could;

- Supply a few drinks and/or snacks,
- Have a group hug, or
- Have an informal 'thank you' speech from the event leaders.

In the coming week or two, you could;

- Provide small 'thank you' gifts for the committee,
- Put a notice in the local newspaper,
- Announce the results as broadly as possible, or
- Write 'thank you' letters to supporters, sponsors and committee mentioning the result and the great work of the committee.

You can use as many of these celebrations as you choose to, but there is one other activity that really must be done. It is important to hold a committee meeting about two to three weeks after the event to analyse how everyone feels the event went. These meetings are sometimes called a Post Mortem, Post Event Evaluations, or Mop-Up meetings. What ever you choose to call it, at this meeting a final financial result should be announced and each committee member should have an opportunity to comment on their thoughts for all facets of the event. Typically these meetings are quite relaxed and informal, often being held over a cuppa or even something a little stronger. Some of the best Mop-Up meetings have been held in coffee shops where members can feel relaxed and enjoy the celebration.

The entire process of identifying a cause, identifying the benefits, putting together a committee, running committee meetings, selecting an event, allocating roles, engaging volunteers, completing the tasks, supervising progress, staging the event, and mopping-up afterwards is a very demanding undertaking. Doing all of this with volunteers is an incredible feat. Only a few people in your community would have the abilities required to undertake such a task, fewer still would be capable of getting great results. If you have gone through this whole process successfully then you are a unique and special person and you are a great asset to your community. The reason we do fundraising events is to help needy causes and to make a difference in our community. People will notice your efforts and achievements and they will be thankful for what you and your committee have achieved. You have every right to feel a high level of personal pride with what you and your team have achieved. Well done.

APPENDIX

Appendix 1

Selecting A Fundraising Activity

Selecting an appropriate event for your group to run is never an easy task. Just coming up with a few good ideas can often be quite difficult. This appendix contains a large list of fundraising activities that will ensure that you are never stuck for ideas again. It is just a matter of reading through the list and noting the requirements necessary to run the event. Ensure that you have or can get the requirements listed before you get too attached to an idea.

This list should in no way replace the old way of finding new ideas to bring to your committee; that of brainstorming. Brainstorming is a great way to tap into people's creativeness and you should consider using brainstorming techniques where ever appropriate. If you can't find what you're looking for in this list then brainstorming may help.

Remember that when brainstorming there are two golden rules which must be adhered to;

1. Everybody's ideas are absolutely equal, and
2. No negative comments about any ideas.

After the brainstorming session is over, use the group to remove the ideas which are impractical and then define and refine a core group of ideas for further development.

However you won't need to go through the brainstorming process if you can find what you are looking for right here in this appendix. These ideas have been grouped into four categories;

1. Sell Something
2. Run An Event
3. Run A Business
4. Ask For Help

More information about how to use this appendix is found in Chapter 6—Selecting a Fundraising Event.

SELL SOMETHING

The activities listed in this category have been selected because they involve the sale of something to produce an income.

The items being sold could be new or old, home made or professionally made, donated or purchased, cheap or expensive. Keep in mind that the best profits can be made if the items for sale have been donated to you (either new or used). Major charities often have fundraising events that involve the selling of new novelty merchandise such as a "Red Nose". These activities work well because the major charities have extensive distribution networks and broad public awareness.

There are many different ways and methods for selling things, so consider all options when looking at these activities.

In this category, tables show the following:

Income	= Yearly Income
Planning Time	= Time to Properly Plan the Activity
Committee	= Planning Helpers
Crew	= Activity Helpers

Stalls (at Markets, Fetes etc)

(Trash & Treasure Stall, Craft Stall, Plant Stall, Chocolate Stall, Cake Stall, Produce Stall, Jams Stall, Sausage Sizzles, Bar-B-Ques, etc.)

Income	Planning Time	Committee	Crew
$50-$500	3-6 weeks	3	5

With all these stalls the secret to success is getting the items for the stall produced for free. Get your members to spend some time preparing the items for sale and this will also encourage them to help with the stall on the day.

If you choose to do a plant stall, considerably longer preparation time will be required in order to establish seedlings and get plants established.

You will need to have somewhere to store all the items before the day and you will need some helpers with appropriate vehicles to ferry the products around. With stalls there are minimal overheads, so a tidy profit can be made.

If done weekly at markets, stalls can raise significant funds annually.

Drives

(Chocolate, Bulbs, Pie, Cake, Puddings, Pizza, Family Photos, etc.)

Income	Planning Time	Committee	Crew
$50-$10,000	6-26 weeks	3	3

Sell anything desirable that is highly consumable, that way people will always want more. These activities work best where many participants are readily available as in schools, etc. One of the best results from any drive is always the old reliable chocolate drive. Other types of drives will generally still be successful but raise less money.

Raffles (Minor < $2,000)
(Multi-draw, Chook, Bingo, Meat/Seafood Trays, Wheelbarrow with goods, Money Tree, Scratch Tickets, Lucky Envelopes, Rocking Horse, Heads & Tails, etc)

Income	Planning Time	Committee	Crew
$10-$500	1-4 weeks	2	3

Raffles are still one of the best fundraisers around. They require little planning time and can be done with a very small committee. They are also easy and cheap for the target audience to support.

Many volunteer fundraisers incorporate a raffle into some other gathering when the audience is already available.

Running regular raffles is a great way to achieve really high results. Always try to get the prizes donated if possible.

Raffles (Major >$2,000)
(Car, Boat, Holiday, Trailer with Goods, House, etc.)

Income	Planning Time	Committee	Crew
-$2,000-$100,000	6-26 weeks	3	100

Large raffles are really only for charities or groups with large memberships and/or contacts to help with getting the prizes donated or substantially reduced. I've seen car raffles that were on sale for 6 months, then had to extend the time another 3 months because not enough tickets had been sold to cover the cost of the car. When it was finally drawn the raffle still made a loss. It pays to be very conservative with these types of raffles unless you have a very wide distribution network for the tickets.

Art unions where charities are offering a magnificent home as the prize are less common today than they were 20 years ago. The reason for this is that only a few of the well established charities can actually make a regular profit at it.

Auctions

(Celebrity, Memorabilia, Cent, Art Shows, Art Auctions, Radio/ Internet, First Fruit for the Year, etc)

Income	Planning Time	Committee	Crew
$50-$15,000	8-40 weeks	3	5

Be creative when thinking of something to auction. Consider auctioning the sorts of things that money can't buy. If you can get items donated that are of interest to your audience such as celebrity signed sporting attire, etc, an auction is the best way to maximise the income from them. Auctions are best held with a meal and entertainment, and it will also help considerably with the bidding if alcohol is available at the function. It's not such a silly idea to include alcohol in the ticket price so that the audience will be nicely relaxed by the time for bidding.

Merchandise For Sale

(Red Nose, Daffodils, Bandanas, Pens, etc)

Income	Planning Time	Committee	Crew
Undefined	Undefined	Undefined	Undefined

Gaining popularity with fund raising organisations is to have an item for sale that allows supporters to purchase a branded item which also show the world they donated to your cause. Annual release of these items creates a number number of high value donors who show there support every year. Unique new ideas could do well as long as they are affordable and you have a good distribution method. Only very large organisations should try this idea, as you will need a cheap and unique item distributed very widely to make a profit.

Rides
(Hot Air Balloon, Amusements, Motor Bike, etc)

Income	Planning Time	Committee	Crew
$50-$15,000	6-26 weeks	3	5

Most often these types of activities are held in conjunction with a more major event, i.e. a Show or a Fete. However, it is possible to hold a ride as a stand alone fundraising event. You will need to ensure that you have a unique aspect to your ride and that it can be marketed to the broader public without too much expense.

Second-hand Sales
(Garage, Boot, Farm, etc.)

Income	Planning Time	Committee	Crew
$100-$1,000	4-12 weeks	3	5

If an organization asks its members to donate goods for sale at a Boot Sale or Garage Sale, etc, it can be a quick way to raise some funds. One advantage of these sales is that the group's members get to clear out the old junk from their home as well as help their charity.

RUN AN EVENT

The activities listed in this category have been selected because they involve the staging of an event or activity to produce an income.

The event could be held weekly, monthly, annually or even just once.

One of the main drawbacks to running events is there is always a lot of work required to get all the details organized and when the event is over everything is put away until the next time. This can make running events very demanding and harder to be successful at. Running the same event a number of times may make some of the planning required simpler however you should also keep in mind that you will also need to change the event from year to year in order to keep the event fresh and new.

The main advantage of running events is that the public generally like to attend events. There is a certain thrill that people get from seeing or doing something out of the ordinary and if your event can offer that then it has a good chance of success.

Running events is a pretty competitive sector of fundraising but there are some great opportunities for success here still.

In this category the tables show the following:

Income	=	Yearly Income
Planning Time	=	Time to Properly Plan the Activity
Committee	=	Planning Helpers
Crew	=	Activity Helpers

-A-Thons
(Walk, Swim, Sleep, Sail, Ride, Skate, Read, Spell, Skip, Pole Sitting, etc)

Income	Planning Time	Committee	Crew
$500-$15,000	10-26 weeks	3	5

These events have long been the corner stone of school fundraising efforts. That's because they perform best with a large crew who are motivated to go out and get financial support from individual 'sponsors'. When the income from each participant is combined, it can often add up to a lot of money.

Excursions/Tours
(Winery, Shopping, Fishing, Golfing, etc)

Income	Planning Time	Committee	Crew
$50-$3,000	6-26 weeks	2	2

Put on a bus trip to an interesting and fun venue. Charge a bit more than the total costs to make a profit. Promote it to the people who would support your cause and would enjoy the theme of your excursion. The number of commercial excursion providers is expanding rapidly in Australia which reflects its growing popularity. You could do raffles and other fundraisers in the bus along the way.

Car Rally
(Local, Long Distance, Mystery Tours, etc)

Income	Planning Time	Committee	Crew
$200-$50,000	6-52 weeks	5	5

A small local rally is just a matter of getting your club members to enter for a small fee. They follow a set of cryptic clues (not too hard) till they find the destination. A barbecue and games could be held at the destination. It is illegal to make these rallies a time trial as entrants would be encouraged to speed. Instead, time the trip driving straight from the start to the finish going at the speed limit and then deduct points from entrants who come in faster or slower than the official time.

Bigger rallies have large entry fees and professionally fitted out vehicles and can go for quite long distances over several days or weeks. A lot of planning is required if you want to attempt a big car rally but they can be very successful once established and are usually a lot of fun too.

Entertainment Nights
(Theatre, Cinema, Fashion Parades, Card Party, Games Night, Pajama Party, Garden Party, Red Faces, Trivia Nights, Murder Parties, Karaoke, etc)

Income	Planning Time	Committee	Crew
$50-$2,000	6-26 weeks	4	5

These nights are basically an excuse for a party with a strong fundraising component. Your audience will be more than happy to part with some cash for a good cause if they are having fun as well. Money can be raised by an entry fee and raffles, etc.

Cinemas and Theatres may offer group discounts to charity events which mean that the organisers can make a profit if they charge the participants full fee. Sometimes pre-release showings are available and these can be very attractive to audiences.

Sometimes fashion parades are an 'add-on' for other events, but sometimes they can be run on their own. If you have an interesting theme and a good location, people will be very willing to attend. Invite the sort of people who would be most likely to enjoy the parade theme, i.e. latest modern fashions—young women, business suits—professional women, children's wear—young mums, etc.

Dances
(Social, Disco, Western, etc)

Income	Planning Time	Committee	Crew
$500-$3,000	6-26 weeks	5	10

Choose a theme, organise some good music and a venue, advertise the event and that's about all there is to running a dance. The reputation of the music and the venue will have a large bearing on the number of people who attend it. When running a dance for under-age children a LOT of supervision and responsibility is required. You would need to check your liability exposure should something go wrong and you will also need all adults working at the dance to have a Blue Card.

Theme Meals
(Corporate, Ladies, Melbourne Cup, Long Lunch, Sporting, Progressive Dinners, Champagne Breakfasts, International Food & Beer, etc)

Income	Planning Time	Committee	Crew
$500-$5,000	6-26 weeks	5	10

With the right committee these events can be run quite smoothly. Two of the keys to the success of these activities are having a high quality speaker and a high profile beneficiary. It is also better to book a smaller venue which will be full, rather than a larger one that is only half full. Maybe have an auction, raffle or fashion parade with it also to create an additional income stream.

Fun Sports
(Ten Pin Bowling, Horse Trail Ride, Skating, Sailing, Skiing, Golf, Lawn Bowls, Motor Boat, Jet Ski, Fun Runs/Walks, Mini Olympics, Family Fun Day, Community Sports, Bed Push, etc)

Income	Planning Time	Committee	Crew
$500-$5,000	6-26 weeks	5	10

Advertise for teams to enter a fun day of sports. Prepare a series of competitive events but with the emphasis on anyone can win. You can charge a fee for the teams and maybe a small entry fee for spectators but the entrants should be encouraged to seek sponsorship for their entry.

These types of events can be organised and run by one volunteer however better results are usually achieved when they are organised by an active committee. Many sporting venues are very experienced at these types of events, so if you contact them you should get a lot of guidance and direction.

When the public support a community group to raise funds, they often like to get a good feeling as a result. A fun sports event gives people that good feeling. This type of event will almost certainly need to be advertised to get sufficient participants. As always, a great prize will help get people involved.

Contests
(Sports, Camp Draft, Rodeo, Triathlon, Bike Race, etc.)

Income	Planning Time	Committee	Crew
$50-$3,000	6-26 weeks	5	10

These events are capable of being run just for your group or they can be open to the public. Whichever way you choose to run them though, the key element here is competition. These events are about the performers putting on a competitive show for the audience to enjoy watching.

Contests are quite popular fundraising activities because many competitive sports teams need to fundraise. You need to organise the competitors, prizes, venue, equipment, etc. Profits are often increased by selling food and drinks or holding a raffle or auction with it as well.

Quests
(Junior, Miss, Golden, Baby, Bar Attendant, Nurse, Community, etc.)

Income	Planning Time	Committee	Crew
$1,000-$500,000	6-26 weeks	5	5

It is quite common for established fundraising organisations to already run a quest of some type. This is not only a good fundraiser but also great for increasing your visibility and profile within the community. It will however, take a lot of work to recruit entrants and also to stage the gala awards night. Quests can be run on a smaller scale but creating a vibrant and energetic awards night with less entrants and less guests in attendance can be quite a challenge.

Balls
(Deb, Gala, Theme, etc.)

Income	Planning Time	Committee	Crew
$500-$5,000	6-26 weeks	5	10

This is a good event to raise your profile with the 'right' people and can be a lot of fun as well. These events appeal to a very specific market; the 'top end of town', which is highly desirable market to promote your cause to. However this market is also highly selective about what events they attend so your ball will need to have special appeal.

Much of the profit of the night is made from the entry fee which therefore must be substantially higher than the cost price in order to make a profit. Keep an eye on the expenses because they can get out of hand with a ball. The catering, band, venue, and promotional costs will all be quite substantial which will mean that you will have to get a certain number of tickets sold in order to break even. Try to keep this number to less than half of what you expect to achieve.

The secret to attracting guests to a ball is, as usual, that both the cause and the event must be important to the target market.

Washes
(Dog, Car, Truck, Houses, etc.)

Income	Planning Time	Committee	Crew
$50-$300	3-10 weeks	3	10-20

Rules now govern the locations where washes can be done in order to minimize the environmental impact of the harmful chemicals, so check the requirement for approvals first with your local council. These are good activities for youth groups and church groups. You will need a large crew of helpers who are prepared to work well together.

Best run on a Saturday at a popular service station or shopping centre but don't get too excited about making much money from a wash. Remember to set the goal for your income before you choose a fundraising event. Doing a wash will produce a quick hundred or two but don't expect much more than that.

Festivals
(Music, Local Attraction, Local Produce, Themed, etc.)

Income	Planning Time	Committee	Crew
$500-$50,000	16-40 weeks	10	10-20

Most of us would be aware of the successful festivals in our local areas. Jazz festivals, food festivals, fruit festivals, flower festivals, and wine festivals are just some in my own local region. Getting the cause and the event right here is very important and remember that all large successful festivals started small and grew to be large over time.

Shows
(Car, Agricultural, Yacht, Trade, Caravan & Camping, Airplanes, Swap Meet, Dog, Doll/Teddy, Baby, Magic Show, etc.)

Income	Planning Time	Committee	Crew
$1,000-$20,000	52 weeks	10	10-20

These are usually much bigger events usually reserved for commercial event organization or very strong volunteer groups. They do take a lot of planning and should get easier to plan after a number of years when the process has been established and refined. They can produce very substantial and reliable income but are still vulnerable to threats such as external competition and changing market trends, etc.

Concerts
(Opera, Jazz, Celebrity Performers, etc)

Income	Planning Time	Committee	Crew
$1,000-$20,000	40 weeks	10	10-20

These events are very similar to shows (above) and those comments are valid here also. A unique twist, such as doing the concert in unusual venues will encourage ticket sales.

Expos
(Antique Fairs, Hobby Expos, Schools Expos, Car & Boat, Garden Expos, etc.)

Income	Planning Time	Committee	Crew
$1,000-$50,000	52 weeks	10	10-20

These events are very similar to shows (above) and those comments are valid here also.

RUN A BUSINESS

The activities listed in this category have been selected because they are usually day to day activities as opposed to the other three categories where the activities are usually only run occasionally.

Fundraising has evolved over time from simple donation seeking to the current array of very complex activities that we have today. One of the more complex fundraising concepts available today is to run a business. Profitable businesses can be managed just as effectively by capable volunteers as they can by paid staff.

Volunteer groups which choose to run a business need to ensure they are not distracted by other tasks and therefore should either be solely tasked with the management responsibility of the business or they should establish a sub-committee which is solely tasked with the management responsibility. These activities are just too critical for a committee to have other tasks as well.

In this category the tables show the following:

Income   = Yearly Income
Time   = Monthly Management Hours
Committee   = Management Committee
Crew   = Staff Pool (either paid or voluntary)

Ownership/Management Rights

(Museums, Tourist Attractions, Halls, Book Shop, Used Clothing Shop, etc.)

Income	Operational Time	Committee	Crew
$500-$50,000	5-200 hours/month	8	4-40

Operating the management rights for a facility is actually undertaken by more volunteer groups than you might think. Councils and governments often like to have a community group involved in managing some of their facilities such as halls, museums, art galleries, tourist attractions, etc. If you are thinking you would like to run a business such as this, you will need to proactively approach your council and government departments. You should also consider approaching existing managers of these facilities as sometimes they are hoping for a way out of the management rights and are just waiting to be approached.

Property Developers
(Sell, Rent, etc.)

Income	Operational Time	Committee	Crew
$10,000-$100,000	20-60 hours/month	8	0

Not many volunteer organizations get involved in this activity as the risks are really quite high and the expertise required is quite rare. The idea though is to acquire some property, develop it and then sell or rent it. The development of the property is usually done using contractors who donate some or all of their time and materials.

Providing Labour
(Tuck Shop, Clothing Pools, Security, Car Parking, Phone Book Distribution, Pamphlet Distribution, Supermarket Stocktake, Waiters, Mowing, etc.)

Income	Operational Time	Committee	Crew
$5,000-$20,000	2-10 hours/month	6	20-40

If your club has a specific facility or skill, sometimes people are prepared to pay to access them. Schools do well out of tuck-shops, clothing pools, etc. Maybe you could provide labour to erect tents, direct traffic at a large event, or provide waiters at large dinners. You can make a handy profit out of providing a service where your labour costs are free.

Markets (Street/Park)
(Trash & Treasure, Farm Produce, Niche Products, White Elephants, etc.)

Income	Operational Time	Committee	Crew
$5,000-$40,000	10-30 hours/month	6	10-20

Markets have made some community groups a lot of money over the years. Once established, a regular and popular market will provide a steady cash flow for your group. The challenge here is that this industry is quite mature these days and finding a way to enter a highly competitive industry can be quite difficult.

Billeting
(Students, Farmers, etc.)

Income	Operational Time	Committee	Crew
$2,000-$6,000	20-50 hours/month	3	20-50

A number of overseas students come to Australia each year as part of our strong educational tourism market. They pay well to be billeted into Australian Homes. This activity has the added bonus of being a cultural experience for all concerned.

Catering at Events
(Chips, Drinks, Ice Cream, Burgers, etc.)

Income	Operational Time	Committee	Crew
$5,000-$25,000	5-10 hours/month	3	5-20

Buy or hire a food van and have your members staff it regularly at major events. If you have strong support this could even be done at monthly or weekly events. Keep a close eye on the amount of non-returnable food or drinks purchased for the event as this will cut into the profits.

ASK FOR HELP

The activities listed in this category have been selected because they involve asking people and organizations for financial support without offering anything tangible in return.

This type of fundraising probably originated from begging and despite that negative image, it has developed into a very successful segment of the industry. If your cause is a really worthy one then people will always be willing to donate to it. Some of the most successful individual fundraisers achieve their results by just asking for donations. It is not complicated and anyone can do it. The better you get at it, the better the results will be.

You will see that there are many different ways of asking for money so don't limit your imagination here. In fact new ideas are often rewarded where old ideas are being spurned. Asking for donations can be renewed and invigorated just like everything else.

Seeking grants from funding bodies fits into this category and, if done properly can reap absolutely incredible results and perform better than many other types of fundraising. Funding bodies frequently apply certain conditions so ensure that you meet your obligations and you may be in a good position to receive further support again.

In this category the tables show the following:

Income   = Yearly Income
Planning Time   = Time to Properly Plan the Activity
Committee   = Planning Helpers
Crew   = Activity Helpers

Donations
(Dress Down Days, Coin Trail, etc.)

Income	Planning Time	Committee	Crew
$100-$2,000	6 weeks	3	3

You could just ask people to donate but now days there are some novel ways of getting people to donate rather than just asking for the money. Holding a coin trail where people place a coin on the ground next to the preceding one leads to a long line of coins.

A dress down day is just a donation. If your school P&C wants to do a dress down day in your school only, it's as easy as telling everybody when it's on and then collecting the money. However if your target audience for a dress down day is the general public then you will need to do considerably more planning to make it successful and the costs will be higher.

Kidnap Celebrities
(Sporting, Politicians, Business and Community Leaders, etc.)

Income	Planning Time	Committee	Crew
$3,000-$15,000	6 -16 weeks	5	5

This is one of the relatively new ideas around that has already been shown to be successful. It is an idea that should not be used too often though because the public is likely to tire of it fairly quickly. It works by getting well connected people to phone their family, friends and acquaintances with a personal plea to donate in order to be released. The mechanism of their entrapment is open to your imagination.

Hair Clips

Income	Planning Time	Committee	Crew
$500-$100,000	6-52 weeks	5	5-50

A unique way of getting money out of peoples pockets is to have people solicit sponsorship from their family, friends and acquaintances to shave or colour their hair. These are very successful fundraisers for certain charities which have established themselves in this area.

Request Letters
(Individual, Charity, Mover & Shaker, etc.)

Income	Planning Time	Committee	Crew
$100-$30,000	1-10 weeks	3	0

Request letters can be initiated by a single person writing to local businesses, the charity itself sending letters out to its database of supporters, or from a mover & shaker who may be a head of a company who writes to his suppliers and colleagues asking them to help support his charity. No matter who initiates the letter or who it goes to, the letter will perform better when there is a highly emotional plea attached to a highly urgent cause.

Doorknocks

Income	Planning Time	Committee	Crew
$10,000-$500,000	16-40 weeks	6	20-1,000

Doorknocks are an old concept and are not as successful as they used to be. Doorknocks take a lot of planning and huge numbers of crew prepared to help on the day but for major charities they can still produce some very important funds each year.

Collection Tins
(Shop Counter, Public Place, etc)

Income	Planning Time	Committee	Crew
$100-$1,000	1-12 weeks	3	5-50

Many charities and causes have tried the shop counter collection tin. Unfortunately they are a passive type of fundraising and do not usually raise much money. If the shop attendants are supportive of the cause and are prepared to solicit donations from their customers, they may do a little better.

Collection tins work better if there is a person holding on to them and they work better again if that person is a vibrant happy person willing to talk to people about the cause. If you undertake one of these activities try to have many collectors spread over a large area like in a shopping centre or a sporting venue. If the venue is prepared to support the collection with public announcements then the collection will be much more successful.

Appeals
(Gifts, Toys, Blankets, etc.)

Income	Planning Time	Committee	Crew
$0 (Items are donated)	8-16 weeks	8	10 -20

Appealing to the public to donate items for a specific cause is not really a fund raiser because it doesn't raise any funds but it does help provide much needed items. This can sometimes help an organisation meet its goals just as much as cash. Of course the items donated must be required by the organisation or sold separately and converted to cash.

Grants
(Council, State Govt., Fed Govt., Gaming Funds, Foundations, etc.)

Income	Planning Time	Committee	Crew
$50-&100,000	4-26 weeks	3	0

Some granting bodies have a reasonably simple application form available which makes applying very easy, whilst others require a great deal of expertise and knowledge.

The big dollars on offer make it worth the effort to apply for a grant if you have somebody available with the expertise necessary to prepare a solid submission. This is a highly competitive area and the granting body will have many submissions to choose from. The secret to success here is selecting a project for funding that exactly matches their granting purpose, demonstrating a strong need for the item requested and proving your organisation has the skills to manage the project effectively.

Appendix 2

Budget

Item	Comments	Income	Expenses	Result
School Fete -Budget				
Stalls				
22 Stalls Income	22 x $600	$13,200		$13,200
Calico banners	46m x $2		$92	-$92
Table/chair hire	Donated			$ -
Teacher Dunk Machine			$50	-$50
Balloons			$300	-$300
Entertainment				
Sponsors	1 x $500	$500		$500
Stage hire	School Eqpt.			$ -
PA hire	School Eqpt.		$ -	$ -
Music amp/ microphone hire			$100	-$100
Amusements				
Jumping Castle	400x$2	$800	$640	$160
Giant Slide	400x$2	$800	$640	$160

Mini Cars	400x$3	$1,200	$960	$240
General				
Promotion	Internal		$ -	$ -
Signage			$200	-$200
Insurance	P&C policy		$ -	$ -
Bins	Donated		$ -	$ -
Photography	Donated		$ -	$ -
Gifts for helpers			$100	-$100
Container hire	Storage		$112	-$112
TOTAL		**$16,500**	**$3,194**	**$13,306**

Appendix 3

Promotional Flyer

Verysmart State School

SCHOOL FETE

Saturday 11th November
11:00am till 4:00pm

The theme this year is the 18th century complete with Horse and Buggy rides.

Free Entry

Activities to look forward to are; fun rides, slides, class performances, dance demonstrations, 22 stalls, music, 18th century dresses, horse drawn carriages, plus much more....

A great day out for all the family, bring along your Mum, Dad, Brothers, Sisters, Grand Parents, Uncles, Aunts and Neighbours.

Held at the school
101 Verylong St,
Verybigsville.

Appendix 4

'To Do' List

School Fete—To Do List				
Line items highlighted in Grey have been completed.				
Task	**Date**	**Organiser**	**Status**	**Comments**
Class Stalls				
Appoint class stalls coordinator	ASAP	Darren		
Ensure availability of stall frames	Sep	Susan	Done	
Book marquees and tents	1 May	John P		
Ensure/book tables & chairs	1 Jun	Susan		
Prepare list of stall ideas	1 May	Committee		
Seek class convenors	1 May	Melanie		
Allocate stalls to classes		Melanie		
Seek donations of supplies	Ongoing	Committee		
Assist convenors with stall planning	Ongoing	Melanie		
Ensure sufficient money pouches	3 Sep	Adrian		
Produce class banner in keeping with the theme	24 Oct	Teachers		
Arrange for pick-up/return, erection/pack-up of; tents, stall frames, tables/chairs, & other eqpt	19 Oct	Alex		
Supervise stalls erection & pack-up	Fete Day	Susan		

Entertainment				
Appoint entertainment coordinator	ASAP	Roxanne		
Book stage	1 May	Roxanne		
Book PA & music amp	ASAP	Roxanne		
Arrange sports/dance/cultural entertainment	1 Aug	Lucy		Karate/ Jazz Ballet/ Gymnastics/ Other?
Arrange an MC	1 Aug	Roxanne		
Arrange class entertainment	28 Sep	Lucy		
Arrange stage schedule	12 Oct	Roxanne		
Amusements				
Appoint amusements coordinator		Darren	Done	
Get quotes for amusements		Tanya	Done	
Decide on amusement requirement		Committee	Done	Slide/Castle/ Jeeps
Negotiate best conditions from amusement vendor		Tanya	Done	20% - armbands
Book amusements	25 Nov	Tanya	Done	
Set prices for amusements		Committee		
Supervise amusements at the fete		Tanya		
Organize ticket sales at/before the fete		Louise		
General				
Form committee	Nov	P&C	Done	
Select date & venue	Nov	P&C	Done	25th October
Hold timely committee meetings	Ongoing	Darren		
Keep meeting minutes & budget	Ongoing	Darren		
Report to P&C on progress	Ongoing	Darren		

Produce information newsletters	Bi-Monthly	Louise		
Decide on the theme for the fete	Apr	Committee		
Supply banner material to class teachers	Sep	Louise		
Review Workplace Health & Safety issues	Ongoing	Darren		
Ensure sufficient promotion	1 Oct	Kym		
Ensure sufficient signage	1 Oct	John L		
Arrange a photographer	1 Oct	John L		
Design layout of fete area	19 Oct	Darren		
Ensure sufficient insurance (indemnity/rainy day)	Sep 02	P&C		
Ensure sufficient rubbish bins	19 Oct	John L		Arrange donation??
Ensure sufficient car parking	19 Oct	John L		
Arrange for an electrician	10 Nov	John L		

Appendix 5

Gantt Report

School Fete—GANTT Report													
Task	**Organizer**	Jan	Feb	Mar	Apr	May	Jun	Jul	Aug	Sep	Oct	Nov	Dec
Class Stalls													
Appoint class stalls coordinator	Darren		■										
Ensure availability of stall frames	Susan						■						
Book marquees and tents	John P								■				
Ensure/book tables & chairs	Susan								■				
Prepare list of stall ideas	Committee			■									
Seek class convenors	Melanie				■	■							
Allocate stalls to classes	Melanie					■							
Seek donations of supplies	Committee							■	■	■	■	■	■
Assist convenors with stall planning	Melanie							■	■	■	■	■	
Ensure sufficient money pouches	Adrian											■	
Produce class banner in keeping with the theme	Teachers											■	
Arrange for pick-up/ return, erection/pack-up of; tents, stall frames, tables/chairs, & other eqpt	Alex												■

Task	Responsible
Supervise stalls erection & pack-up	Susan

Entertainment

Task	Responsible
Appoint entertainment coordinator	Darren
Book stage	Roxanne
Book PA & music amp	Roxanne
Arrange sports/dance/cultural entertainment	Lucy
Arrange an MC	Roxanne
Arrange class entertainment	Lucy
Arrange stage schedule	Roxanne

Amusements

Task	Responsible
Appoint amusements coordinator	Darren
Get quotes for amusements	Tanya
Decide on amusement requirement	Committee
Negotiate best conditions from amusement vendor	Tanya
Book amusements	Tanya
Set prices for amusements	Committee
Supervise amusements at the fete	Tanya
Organise ticket sales at/before the fete	Louise

General

Task	Responsible
Form committee	P&C
Select date & venue	P&C
Hold timely committee meetings	Darren

Task	Responsible
Keep meeting minutes & budget	Darren
Report to P&C on progress	Darren
Produce information newsletters	Louise
Decide on the theme for the fete	Committee
Supply banner material to class teachers	Louise
Review Workplace Health & Safety issues	Darren
Ensure sufficient promotion	Kym
Ensure sufficient signage	John L
Arrange a photographer	John L
Design layout of fete area	Darren
Ensure sufficient insurance	P&C
Ensure sufficient rubbish bins	John L
Ensure sufficient car parking	John L
Arrange for an electrician	John L

Appendix 6

Promotional Plan

School Fete—Promotional Plan		
Verysmart State School 101 Verylong St, Verybigsville Saturday 11th November 11:00 am till 4:00 pm		
Item	**Target**	**Distribution Date**
School Parade Announcements	School Students	2 x July 2 x August 4 x September 4 x October 3 x November
Fliers	School Parents	11th October
Fliers	Local Homes	3rd November
Media Release	Local Newspaper	3rd November
Media Release	Local Radio	3rd November

Appendix 7

Run Sheet

School Fete—Run Sheet			
Verysmart State School			
101 Verylong St, Verybigsville			
Saturday 11th November			
11:00 am till 4:00 pm			
Time	**Activity**	**Person**	**Notes**
9:00am	School Grounds open for setup	Groundsman	
9:00am	Stalls set up	Melanie	Will need 5 helpers with hammers
9:00am	Stage set up	Roxanne	Will need 1 assistant
9:00	Amusement set up	Tanya	Ensure they follow the layout plan
9:00am	Electricity provided to stalls/Stage/Amusements	Electrician	Will need 1 helper
10:00am	Amusements ticket sales begin	Amusement Vendors	Amusement Coordinator to supervise

10:45am	Cash floats delivered to Stalls	Adrian	Will need two helpers
11:00am	Rides/Entertainment/ Stalls begin	Amusement Vendors	Amusement Coordinator to supervise
11:00am	Bar-b-que opens	Barry	Grade 3C stall
	Entertainment Schedule		
11:00am	Official Opening	MC Intro Darren & Principal	Thank sponsors / committee
11:15am	Performance 1	MC Intro	Grade 1
11:45pm	Performance 2	MC Intro	Grade 2
12:15pm	Performance 3	MC Intro	Grade 3
12:45pm	Demonstration 1	MC Intro	School Orchestra
1:00pm	Demonstration 2	MC Intro	School Choir
1:15pm	Demonstration 3	MC Intro	4 Solos
1:30pm	Performance 4	MC Intro	Grade 4
2:00pm	Performance 5	MC Intro	Grade 5
2:30pm	Performance 6	MC Intro	Grade 6
3:00pm	Performance 7	MC Intro	Grade 7
3:30pm	Demonstration 4	MC Intro	School Band
4:00pm	Draw Raffles and Close	MC & Darren	Thank student /parents/ sponsors / committee
4:05pm	Pack up	Everyone	
Note			
Times listed are a guide only.			

References

1. Philanthropy Australia website—
    http://www.philanthropy.org.au/research/factsheets/PA_
    volunteeringaus.pdf

2. Australian Bureau of Statistics website—2001 Census
    Tables—Australia, Industries of Employment by
    Occupation—Australia.

3. 'The Australian Guide to Chairing Meetings' by Marjorie
    Puregger, 1998, Chapter 4 Motions and Amendments.

4. The Cambridge Dictionaries Online
    http://dictionary.cambridge.org/define.asp?key=48897&dict
    =CALD

5. The Australian Bureau of Meteorology website—
    http://www.bom.gov.au/climate/averages/tables/cw_
    041103.shtml